Shibori

For Textile Artists

Shibori

For Textile Artists

Janice Gunner

To Sue
Enjoy!.
Janice Gunner

BATSFORD

Dedication

To my husband David, together with my sons David, Nicolas and James for putting up with textiles all over the house, late meals and senior moments!

This edition published in 2018 by
Batsford, an imprint of Pavilion Books Company Ltd
43 Great Ormond Street
London
WC1N 3HZ

First published in the United Kingdom in 2006

ISBN-13: 9781849945301

A CIP catalogue record for this book is available from the British Library.

10 9 8 7 6 5 4 3 2 1

Reproduction by Anorax Imaging Ltd, Leeds
Printed by Toppan Leefung Printing Ltd, China

This book can be ordered direct from the publisher at the website: www.pavilionbooks.com, or try your local bookshop.

All textiles and quilts by the author unless stated otherwise.

Contents

Introduction 6

Chapter 1 Shibori – history and meaning 10

Chapter 2 Tied-resist designs 28

Chapter 3 Stitched-resist designs 40

Chapter 4 Arashi shibori 66

Chapter 5 Itajime – folded and bound/clamp-resist 78

Chapter 6 Tesuji shibori – pleated and bound 86

Chapter 7 Dyeing techniques 98

Chapter 8 Shibori sampler wall hanging 114

Acknowledgements 124

Bibliography 125

Suppliers 126

Index 127

Introduction

As a teenager, in the late 1960s and early 1970s, I experimented with tie-dyeing T-shirts and fabrics. Many a happy hour was spent tying stones and pebbles into fabric and then immersing the whole bundle into cold water dye. The resulting effects intrigued me! Little did I realise it then, but those experiments were just the beginning of my fascination with patterning and colouring textiles.

I have always stitched in some form or another embroidery, dressmaking and patchwork mostly. I love the tactile nature of fabric and this eventually led me to the world of quilting. Once my youngest son started school full time, I decided it was time to launch myself on a series of patchwork and quilting courses. I studied City & Guilds Part 1 & 2, followed by the

below and below right
Traditional *kanoko* shibori cloths using tied resist. The two kimono wraps (*obi age*) are 'linked dot' shibori, the brown and blue cloths are 'square ring dots'; silk, Japan.

Diploma in Stitched Textiles. It was during these courses that I was re-introduced to various methods of dyeing my own fabric and where, during the Diploma, I studied shibori in greater depth. My final pieces for exhibition were all made using *arashi* shibori (see page 66).

The effects that can be achieved from stitching, folding, pleating, tying and clamping designs and patterns into fabric are quite magical. The excitement of releasing the fabric from these techniques after the dyeing process is addictive. Each piece is a surprise, a unique piece of cloth that sets the creative juices flowing – in my case, as a quilter, constantly calling 'Quilt me, quilt me!'

Shibori is the wonderful world of stitched and tied resist-dyed textiles. Let me introduce you to some of these techniques, dyeing methods and ways of using the resulting fabrics. Let the journey begin.

left Antique shibori, tied resist dyed using two or three dye colours for space-dyed effect; silk, Japan.

top right Stitched resist shibori; indigo dyed cotton, purchased at the Arimatsu Shibori Museum, Japan.

bottom right Tied shibori; indigo dyed cotton *yukata* cloth by Ken-ichi Utsuki, Koyoto, Japan.

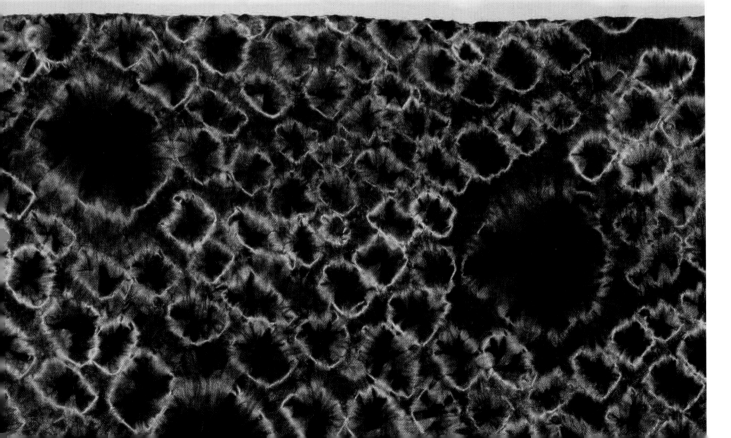

Shibori – history and meaning

Shibori, now a universal term, is the Japanese word for manipulating fabric before dyeing (the word is derived from the Japanese root verb *shiboru*, which means to 'wring, squeeze, press'), and it has become synonymous with many forms of resist-dyed fabric. I find the best way to describe shibori to the uninitiated is as 'sophisticated tie-dyed or stitched-resist fabrics'. I will begin with a short history of shibori in Japan but, as you will soon find out, the technique is not unique to Japan. Similar techniques have been found in many cultures around the world, including Africa, China, Europe, India, Indonesia, Korea, Malaya, and both North and South America. It is known by many other names, some of which I have detailed in this chapter to whet your appetite.

Japan

The technique of shibori in Japan dates back to between the 6th and 8th centuries, where it was probably learned from the Chinese. Early examples of tied and bound resist (*kokechi*), were found preserved in the wooden store house of the great Buddhist temple Todaiji. Possessions of the former Emperor Shōmu were donated by the Empress after his death in AD756 and remain there today. Having been protected from Japan's humid climate, they are among the earliest existing samples of resist-dyed cloth.

Eventually Kyoto became the focus for development in Japanese style and art. Court dress involved many-layered robes of silk, each one dyed in a different shade or colour, references to which can be seen in paintings from the period, and Shibori flourished.

As the centuries progressed stitched-resist began to be used as a method of creating stylised motifs and the use of shibori on clothing spanned all classes. Country people used the techniques to pattern fabrics such as hemp and cotton, dyed with indigo, while silk was still the preserve of the higher classes.

In the early 17th century, the settlement of Arimatsu was established on the eastern coastal route known as the Tokaido, connecting the capitals of Edo and Kyoto. Settlers began producing *tenugui* (small, all-purpose towels) in a bound shibori design. This was the beginning of a thriving village industry that survives to this day. That first pattern was a variation of a design called *kumo* ('spider web') that has been used for centuries and has been made famous by the Arimatsu shibori artists. A special hook was devised that holds the fabric while the thread is wrapped around to make the resist patterning. It is thought that the *yukata* (a light cotton kimono, made with shibori patterned cloth) originated from Arimatsu, as did enlarged designs placed at one shoulder on *kosode*, a jacket robe with small sleeves.

left Spiral (*rasen* or shell) shibori has been used to pattern this antique silk kimono *obi age* cloth; Japan.

By the 19th century the production of shibori began to decline. In 1868 Edo was renamed Tokyo and momentous changes were taking place in Japan. Arimatsu was to lose the market for its shibori, having to compete with other areas producing fabrics using the technique. The fortune of Arimatsu was saved by a man from their own village. Kanezō Suzuki had already originated the shibori method called *shirokage* ('white shadow'), and, on seeing the problems the village faced, devised a new method of wrapping cloth around long poles, pushing it tightly into folds and immersing it into a vat of indigo dye. The method, known as *arashi* ('storm') shibori, was less labour intensive than the others and the production of cloth was dramatically increased. The pattern proved to be popular.

above left Yanagi (willow) shibori, indigo dyed for a summer yukata kimono by Ken-ichi Utsuki, Kyoto, Japan.

right Japanese larch (*karamatsu*) shibori; indigo dyed cotton, stitched resist; Japan.

above Antique *kekka* design, *itajime* (clamp resist) shibori; cotton cloth, fibre reactive dye, Japan.

left *Maki-age* (stitched and tied resist) shibori; cotton cloth, indigo dyed in Japan.

Cloth dyed in Arimatsu was exported to Korea, Taiwan, Singapore and Africa until 1937, and, although trade with Africa was re-established after World War II, changes in post-war Japan seriously affected the demand at home. Shibori was again in danger of becoming a dying art. Japanese women began to wear western-style clothing, only wearing traditional dress for the most formal of occasions, and, as a consequence, many of the younger generations knew little about shibori.

In the early 1980s, shibori was revived as a craft and, as a result, the technique has proved popular and now has universal appeal. Arimatsu is still producing wonderful examples of this ancient art, but it is also moving with the times. Shibori techniques are now being used in so many ways: synthetic fabrics are heat-set using shibori techniques to produce wonderful textured clothes by leading fashion designers. Textile artists, quilters and embroiderers the world over are also using and experimenting with shibori to produce unique fabric for use in their own work. It this interest that ensures the art of shibori is kept alive, both today and for the future.

Africa

West Africa has a strong tradition of tied and stitch-resist-dyed textiles. It can be found in The Gambia, Burkina Faso, Guinea, The Congo (formerly Zaire), Senegal, Mali, Cameroon, Sierra Leone, Cote d'Ivoire and Nigeria. The Kuba people of The Congo tie-dyed the raffia cloth that they wove for clothing, as did the Dida people from Cote d'Ivoire. Very fine *tritik* work, produced by the Soninke and Wolof people along the Senegal river, is embroidery on cloth before being dyed in indigo; when the stitches were removed a negative design was produced, leaving the background blue. Fabrics from The Gambia are often folded to produce striped designs, or scrunched up and dyed to produce a marbled effect.

Indigo is the traditional choice for dyeing fabrics in Africa, although the kola nut (which produces a brown colour) and other brightly coloured dyes are also used.

below A collection of antique African *adire* cloths, indigo dyed; cottons and silk from Gambia, Senegal and Nigeria.

right Indigo and kola nut *adire alabere* from Gambia (also known as *garra* cloth); cotton.

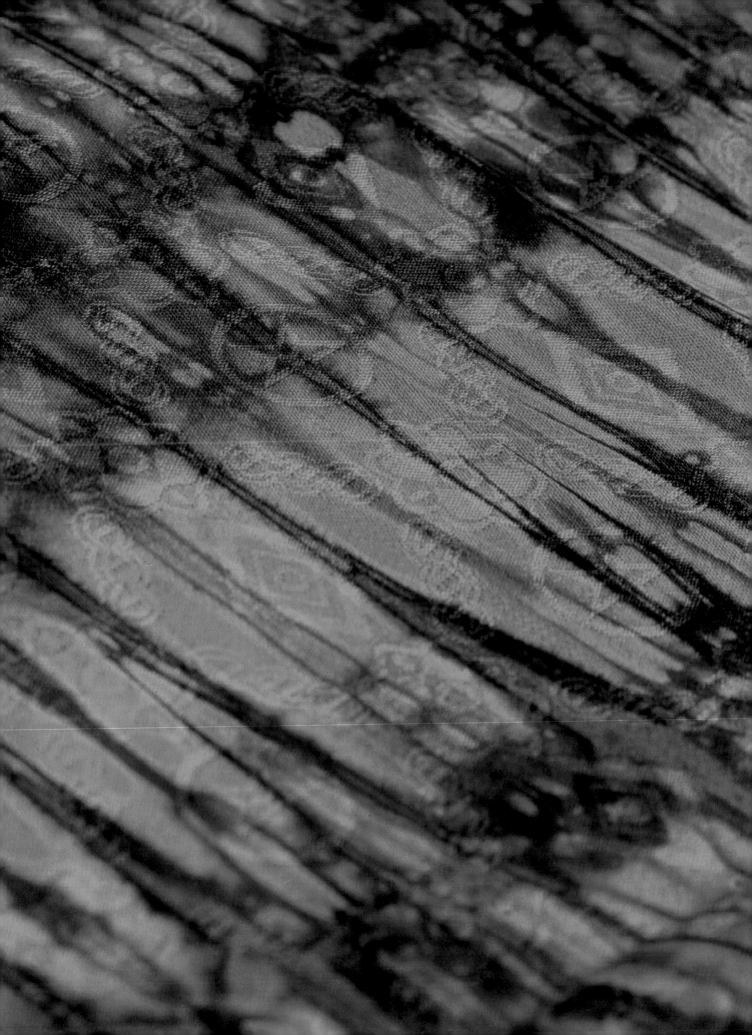

left Pleated and bound *adire alabere* from Gambia; cotton damask cloth, dyed first with fibre reactive dyes and over dyed with indigo.

above Antique *adire oniko* cotton cloth from Nigeria; stitched resist with raphia thread before being indigo dyed.

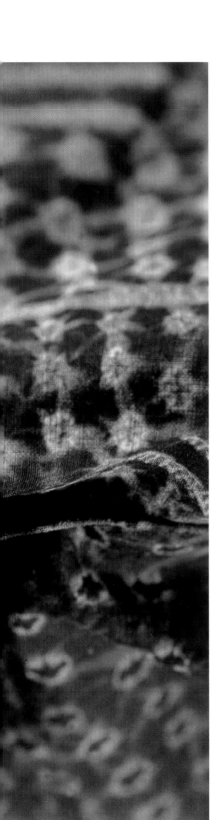

left Antique *adire alabere*
and *oniko* cotton cloth from
Nigeria; stitched with very
fine over sewing and tied
with small circles before
indigo dyeing.

In Nigeria resist-dyed cloth is known as *adire*, with different forms each receiving a suffix according to the method used. Tied cloth is called *adire oniko* – this can either be tied only (sometimes including pebbles or seeds) or folded and tied. Traditionally two or more layers of single-width dampened cloth are tied, or folded and tied at the same time, therefore producing enough cloth to stitch together later for garments (sometimes the fabrics are joined first). The Yoruba people have one of the oldest designs, *osubamaba* ('big moons and little moons') that is still produced today. This design of large circles, tied with as many smaller circles between them as can be fitted in, is worked in raphia, with a finer thread if required for the smaller spots. Folded and tied designs are produced when the dampened fabric is folded into pleats vertically or diagonally and then tied tightly – the ties and folds then resist the dye.

Stitched cloth is known as *adire alabere* and is one of the oldest forms of *adire*. The designs are produced, by layering fabrics as is *adire oniko*, and then stitching by hand or machine. Hand stitching, using raphia or cotton thread (for finer markings), with running or oversewing stitches are used. The fabric is held taut and the stitches are pulled very tight to form the resist. When dyeing is complete, the threads are removed from the dry cloth by cutting with a blade, with the occasional piece of thread left in to prove authenticity. Hand-stitched designs are worked by women.

Machine-stitched *adire* is worked by men, with the designs being similar to those worked by hand, but with much finer stitching. Two cloths are stitched together and folded to give guidelines; the fabric is then stitched using a long stitch length. Simple geometric designs and motifs are used, often done by eye rather than any specific marking. These fabrics are sometimes narrow, only about 7.5 cm (3 in) wide and are joined later with plain strips of fabric to make a larger cloth.

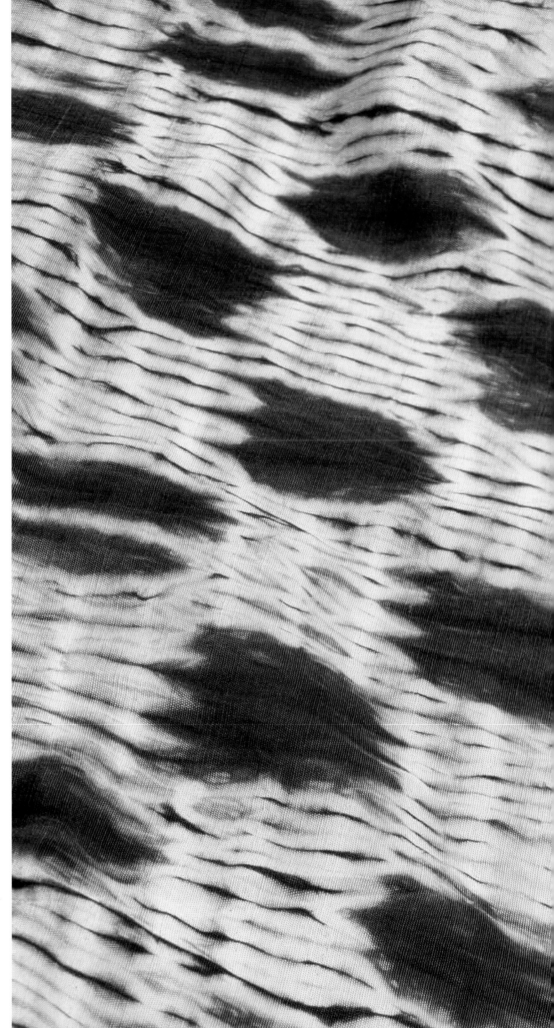

right Antique African silk
cloth, possibly from Senegal,
showing a version of *mokume*,
('wood grain') shibori to form
a chequered design.

left Antique *dida* cloth,
woven from raphia, with
stitched resist motifs.

India

Bandhani is the Indian word for tie-dye, and refers to both the technique and the finished cloth. By pinching and tying the fabric, circular designs are produced, like those in Japanese shibori. The finest *bandhani* are produced in Rajasthan and Gujarat, with coarser variations worked in Sind and Madhya Pradesh.

The simple tied cloths are relatively inexpensive and are used mainly by women in poorer communities. They are brightly coloured, usually with yellow or white dots on deep red backgrounds, and are stunning worn as *odhni* shawls. The finer and more expensive cloths are the preserve of the rich, and consist of many fine knots. These fine *bandhani* shawls made from silk or fine cotton are worn as wedding garments by the women of rich communities in Gujurat.

Bandhani wedding saris consist of a grid of yellow dots against a bright red background with motifs, which include lotus flowers, dancing women and elephants.

Tying the cloth is usually the work of women or young girls. The cloth is either loosely woven silk known as 'georgette' or cotton known as *mal-mal*. Traditionally the white cloth was folded into four or more layers before tying. The dampened cloth was laid out on pins or nails set in wood, and the cloth was then pinched between the nails with thumb and forefinger. This method is now seldom used. Today, one of two methods is used. Either the fabric is marked by a *rangara* (colourer) who dips a cord into a mixture of water-based dye solution containing red ochre, burnt sienna or soot; or a much faster method is used whereby a thin sheet of stiff plastic is pierced with pin holes placed over the fabric and colour sponged or ragged through these to imprint the pattern on the cloth. When this is completed, the tying and dyeing takes place.

The tying is done by pushing the fabric up from behind the dot of colour, usually with the fingernail of the smallest finger or a spiked metal ring, and thread is wrapped around and tied. This thread is then carried onto the next tie, and so on, until all are finished. The fabric is then immersed in the dye, lightest colour first, usually yellow. When the fabric is rinsed, it is re-tied and dyed again with a darker colour, usually red or green, the tied threads covering the previously yellow dyed area. If other darker colours are required, the same process is repeated until all the colours have been dyed. If other spots of colour need to be added, these are usually applied by hand. The finished *bandhani* is sold with the ties still intact to prove that it is genuine.

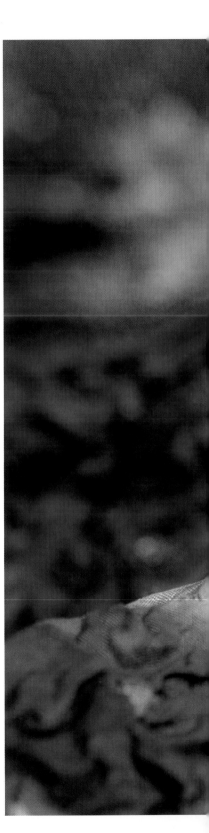

right Indian *Bandhani* shawl with applied sequins and shisha mirrors; polyester fabric.

left Indian *bandhani* scarf of
silk georgette; tied resist with
circular motifs.

above Indian *bandhani*
shawl. The fabric was folded
into four and tied before
dyeing. Additional colours
have been 'spot' applied to
some areas; polyester.

Tied-resist designs

Tied-resist designs and patterns can be found in all of the cultures previously mentioned. Shapes are tied with thread alone or objects are tied into the fabric to make specific shapes or patterns. Traditional Japanese tied designs are usually worked with thread after the fabric has been marked with small dots and then the fabric pinched, or, more commonly, the dot is picked up on a specially made hook that is attached to a stand (*yokobiki dai*); thread is then wrapped around the fabric several times and secured with one or two *kamosage* (half-hitch type) knots. This has the advantage in that the whole cloth can be tied with a series of continually joined knots, which, after dyeing, can be removed by popping them (pulling the fabric taut) to reveal the design. Tying can also be wrapped around the cloth several times, over a longer distance, to make larger designs such as *kumo* ('spider web') shibori.

Tying items into cloth is another way of patterning. I have some African cloth, which has had small items, probably cowrie shells, tied into it to form small oval shapes, but all manner of things could be used. Try small beads, marbles, screws, nuts and bolts and corks. You might think using pulses such as chickpeas would be good, but be warned, they swell in the dye bath and become very difficult to remove – guess how I know!

left Spiral (rasen or shell) shibori design on cotton *yukata* cloth (detail); dyed with indigo, Japan.

below Shibori equipment and cloths prepared for dyeing, showing some of the simple, everyday items that can be used for shibori effects.

left Stitched and tied resist
cotton cloth; indigo dyed,
possibly from China.

above The same piece of cloth,
with the stitching and tying
removed, stretched to reveal
a butterfly design.

You will need:

- Water-soluble marker pen
- Lightweight white cotton fabric – experiment with this first before moving on to other
  natural fabrics such as silk, linen, viscose rayon, silk and viscose velvet, and such like
- Strong cotton or silk thread
- Items to tie in for shaping if you wish

Ne-maki shibori

This is one of the simplest forms of tied resist where the thread is used to pattern the cloth. The
ring shapes that the resist leaves on the fabric can be randomly spaced or more formally placed
by marking before tying.

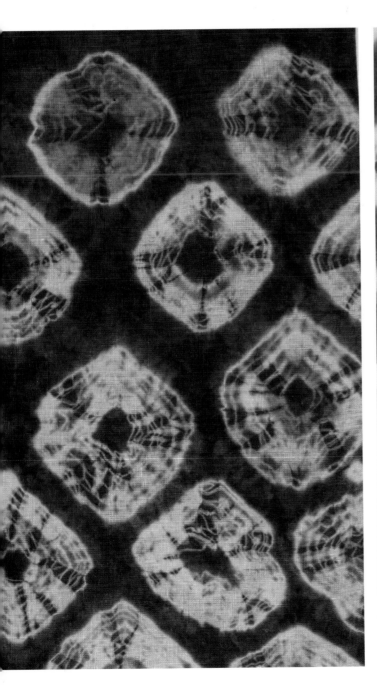

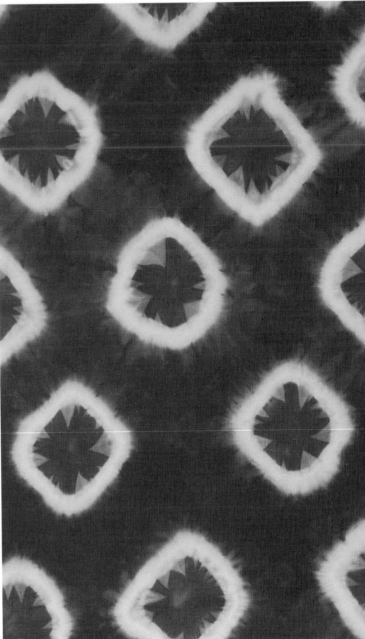

Technique

1. Take a 40 cm (16 in) square of white cotton fabric and mark dots on the fabric, in rows 5 cm (2 in) apart using a water-soluble marker pen.

2. Pinch the first dot of the first row between your thumb and forefinger of your left hand (or right hand if you are left-handed). The *kamosage* knot is not difficult to do, but it will need a bit of practice. Although I have described it here, I have also included some diagrams that I hope will make understanding the following instructions easier (A). Take the end of the thread and hold it tightly with the thumb of this hand against the pinched fabric (B). Rotate the hand so that your thumb and forefinger are twisting the thread back to make a loop (C); slip the loop over the wrapped fabric (D). Secure it by pulling the thread tight at the base of the wrap (E). This may take several attempts to perfect, but persevere, as it will result in a good resist and you will soon get into a rhythm. You may well find your own way of making the knot – so long as it works, keep with it!

3. You should now be able to complete all the dots by moving along and down each row – you don't have to finish off the thread. When you have reached the last dot, take two knots for extra security and cut off the remaining thread (F).

4. Dye your fabric according to your chosen method. Remove the ties when the dyeing process is complete, either before or after washing and drying the fabric.

5. Experiment by tying in found objects such as beads, small shells, screws or plastic corks. Also try tying larger sections of fabric to produce *kumo* ('spider web') shibori, or wrap the thread more than once to achieve the spiral (rasen) shibori design (see page 28).

far left My first attempt at *kumo* ('spider web') shibori using Procion MX dyes and cotton cloth.

left Circles formed by tying glass beads into cotton cloth with rubber bands and using indigo dye.

A

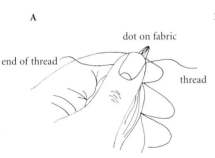

end of thread

dot on fabric

thread

B pass end of fabric under point where thread crosses

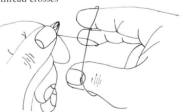

C thread twisted around behind fabric

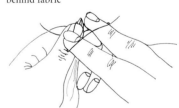

D pull thread tightly to secure

E thread is now pulled tight

F rows of tied dots using *kamosage* knots

Honeycomb shibori

This technique, not strictly traditional shibori, is fun and often surprises people when I show how the fabric is wrapped. The fabric that results, a honeycomb effect that is almost three-dimensional, has a graduated dyed effect with the edge closest to the string the lightest, grading through to dark at the other end. It is especially interesting when it is dyed, re-rolled and then over-dyed again. I usually refer to it as the 'ring doughnut' technique!

Technique

1. Take a 40 cm (16 in) square of white cotton fabric and lay it out flat on the table. Dampen if necessary, depending on your chosen dyeing technique.

2. Now take a 50 cm (20 in) length of string (the thickness of this will determine the size of the honeycomb effect) – I usually use ordinary parcel string or a thick soft cotton yarn. Place the string along the edge of the fabric closest to you. Now fold the edge of the fabric over the string (leaving the extra string protruding from each end). Continue rolling the fabric, not too tightly, around the string until all the fabric is used up.

3. Here comes the fun part. Pick the roll of fabric up and tuck the middle point of the roll under your chin and incline your head to hold the fabric in place! Hold the two ends of the string out in front of you and tie in a reef knot (pulling the gathers tight as you do so), adjust the gathers and finish the knot tightly. What you are left with is a scrunched 'ring doughnut' shape (see below). Don't worry if the edge of the fabric unravels a bit, it will give a darker edge to the finished look.

4. Dye, using the technique of your choice (see pages 98–113). Rinse, and remove the string by cutting close to the knot. Wash and dry the fabric.

above right Honeycomb shibori using Procion MX dyes on cotton cloth and cotton lawn.

below right Indigo dyed honeycomb shibori on cotton sateen cloth, after machine quilting. The fabric has been hand embellished with French knot embroidery using silk thread.

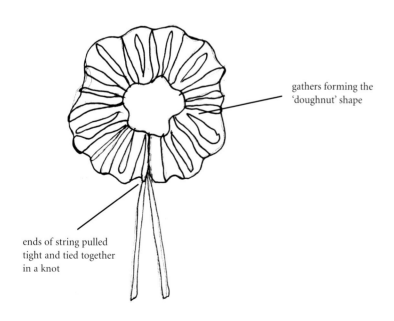

gathers forming the 'doughnut' shape

ends of string pulled tight and tied together in a knot

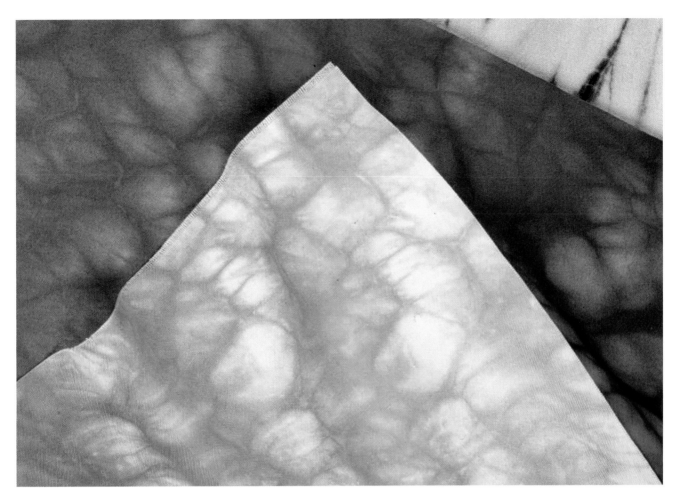

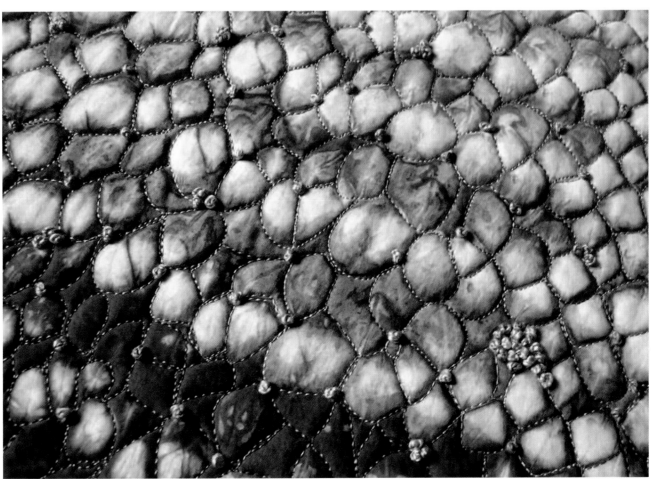

Ideas

- Try the technique out on a plain white T-shirt. By rolling the shirt from the neck edge down, you can achieve a very good effect, especially if you have dyed it with indigo, but remember to dampen the T-shirt first.
- Try re-rolling around a new piece of string, either from the same starting point or the opposite end, and dye again in another colour.

below Crackle shibori (cloth scrunched into a net bag) with indigo dye on cotton poplin.

below Indigo Blues (detail) by Sue Hickman. Shows stitched circles, accentuated with hand and machine quilting, on indigo dyed cloth.

- Try a simple alternative to the honeycomb pattern: scrunch a piece of fabric into a ball and wrap with threads, fine string or rubber bands. You will get a fantastic kind of crackle effect on the fabric when it is dyed, whether with indigo, single colour dye or space dyeing with several colours. I save net bags that hold fruit and vegetables for this technique too. Scrunch the fabric, insert into the net bag, close with a bag clip or rubber band and then dye.

above *Moody Blues* by Cheryl Jackson. A sampler
quilt using a variety of stitched, tied and wrapped
shibori techniques; machine pieced and hand quilted.

below *African Odyssey III* wall hanging using indigo
and kola nut fabrics from Gambia and Nigeria.
Machine pieced and machine- and hand-quilted,
using a variety of threads to add surface texture.

Stitched-resist designs

This chapter will introduce you to the use of stitch on fabric to produce shapes, lines and patterns, one of the most pleasing techniques used in shibori. All sorts of interesting and sometimes complicated designs can be achieved by using the simple stitching methods of running and oversewing stitches. The technique is used in Japanese, African and Indonesian forms of shibori, where it is known respectively as *nui* shibori, *adire alabere* and *tritik*.

The fabric can be stitched as a flat single or double layer, or it can be folded – each method will result in a similar, but different pattern. The shapes can be geometric or organic, single or in rows, and lines can be straight or curved.

Running stitches result in a broken dotted line of resist and oversewing results in a broken diagonal line of resist; the length of the stitches used, whether large or small, will affect the finish too. You can also use your sewing machine to stitch lines of resist; this will produce a more solid line than that of hand stitching. The final result also relies upon which dyeing method you choose to use. Fibre-reactive dyes (such as Procion MX) will give a different result to that of indigo. You may use the technique of dyeing that you prefer. Several methods are described in chapter 7.

Shapes and lines are marked onto the fabric with a water-soluble pen. Use a strong doubled thread; start with a knot, then stitch, and finish by gathering the threads tightly and tying off securely to finish. It is this action that forms the resist. The prepared fabric is now ready to immerse into the dye vat of your choice, and so the magic of shibori begins. Because the dye cannot penetrate through the areas of resist created by the stitching, when the stitching is released after the completion of the dyeing technique, the wonderful patterns, motifs or textures appear!

The following techniques will introduce you to some of the traditional stitched-resist shibori designs. Take time to mark your fabric carefully and use the stitching part of the process as an opportunity to relax! As I stitch, apart from thinking about how I will use the finished fabric, I often think about how I could adapt the design and make it more individual to me. Make notes while any ideas are still fresh in your mind, so they are not so easily forgotten – trust me I know! Experiment – you might never know where it will lead. Try stitching some simple designs on the sewing machine too.

left Indigo stitched resist cotton cloth with wavy line (a variation of Japanese larch) shibori, purchased from the Arimatsu Shibori Museum. Shown with a fine cotton lawn scarf, stitched with squares design and dyed in indigo by Ken-ichi Utsuki, Kyoto, Japan.

You will need:

- Template plastic or card
- Pair of compasses, ruler and pencil
- Paper-cutting scissors
- Water-soluble marker pen
- Lightweight white cotton fabric – experiment with this first before moving on to other natural fabrics such as silk, linen, viscose rayon, silk and viscose velvet; and such like
- Strong cotton thread
- Sewing needle, scissors and thimble

Single layer fabric design:
Mokume shibori ('wood grain')

This is one of my favourite shibori designs, and, to begin with, when stitch is as a resist, one of the easiest to produce.

The parallel lines of stitch, when gathered and dyed, leave a distinctive pattern resembling the effect of wood grain. The length of stitches may vary from row to row, or remain the same throughout the process; what is important, however, is to vary the position of the stitches so that the lines are not rigidly followed. This will give the finished effect a more authentic, organic look. The technique can be speeded up if you are lucky enough to own a smocking/pleater machine, but the finished effect will result in rigid lines of patterning formed by the equidistant spacing of the needles.

right Mokume ('wood grain') shibori; stitched resist on a silk scarf dyed in indigo by Ken-ichi Utsuki, Kyoto, Japan. This detail shows the marks where the fabric was stitched and gathered to make the resist for the design.

Technique

1. Take a 40 cm (16 in) square of white cotton fabric and mark parallel lines across the fabric (warp or weft direction) 2 cm (¾ in) apart.

2. Using a double thread, make a running stitch along the first marked line leaving a long thread to pull up later.

3. Continue in this way, remembering to make sure that you vary the position of all your stitches for an authentic look when finished.

4. Gather up the rows of stitching tightly and knot the ends of thread. At this stage, you may need to cut off some of the excess thread that will have been acquired during the gathering process.

5. Dye your fabric according to your chosen method. Remove the gathers when your dyeing process is complete, either before or after washing and drying the fabric.

Ideas

- Consider experimenting with this technique: try diagonal lines of gathers, wavy lines of gathers or crossed lines. You could dye one colour first and then stitch in the opposite direction, gather and over-dye in another colour.

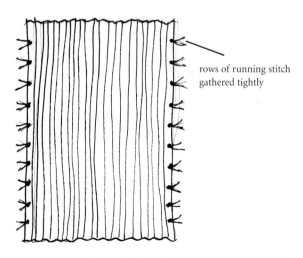

rows of running stitch
gathered tightly

remember to offset stitches in each row
for a more natural wood-grain effect.

right Japanese larch
(*karamatsu*) shibori; cotton
fabric, dyed black. Purchased
from Arimatsu Shibori
Museum, Japan.

Folded cloth designs:
Karamatsu shibori ('larch')

This design consists of alternating rows of consecutive circles: the dark lines within the circles are said to represent the radiating branches of the Japanese native conifer. The design is marked onto folds in the cloth as a half circle; all the rows are then stitched, gathered, secured and dyed.

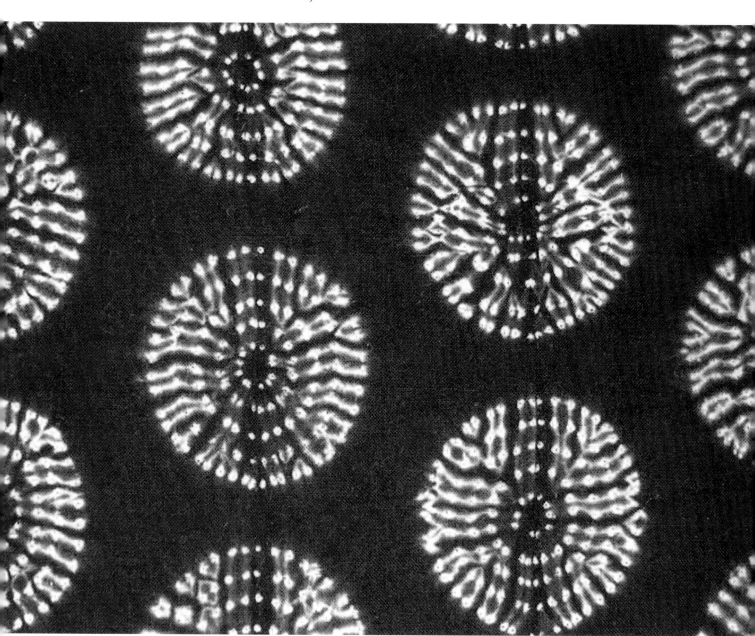

Technique

1. Make three semicircular templates from card or template plastic, using a pair of compasses, in the following sizes:
   - 1 x 5 cm diameter (2 in)
   - 1 x 3.5 cm diameter (1¼ in)
   - 1 x 2 cm (¾ in)

2. Take a 40 cm (16 in) square of white cotton fabric; mark or crease fold lines (along the warp) 5 cm (2 in) apart.

3. Using the templates (largest one first), mark by placing the flat edge of the template along one side of the first marked or folded line. Leave a 2 cm (¾ in) space between each semicircle. Now mark the inner semicircles in the same way, using the medium and small templates.

4. Repeat this stage on the next row, alternating the spacing. Continue in this way until all six rows are marked.

5. Fold the fabric on the first marked or creased line. Using a double thread in your needle, and beginning with a knot, start with the largest semicircular lines marked; work running stitches, one row at a time, across the width of the fabric, taking care to continue the thread across to the next semicircle. At the end of each row, cut the thread, leaving at least 8 cm (3 in) thread hanging (this will be used to draw up the gathers later).

right Variation of the Japanese larch design (*karamatsu*) shibori using alternating semicircles; indigo dyed cotton fabric purchased at Arimatsu Shibori Museum, Japan.

6. Complete each row of semicircles in the same way, taking care not to catch the fabric from the previous rows already stitched.

7. Begin gathering the stitching by carefully pulling the long threads left at the ends of each row. Ease the threads until the gathering is tightly pushed together. Tie off the threads (cut away some of the excess, which by now will have become very long), by dividing the double thread and tying several reef knots to secure tightly. Continue until all gathers are complete in every row.

8. Your fabric is now ready for dyeing, using the method of your choice. Stitching can be removed either before or after the washing and drying processes are complete.

right Stitched rings on a single layer of cotton cloth, Procion MX dye. Note the difference from the folded cloth technique shown on page 45.

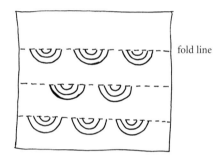

fold line

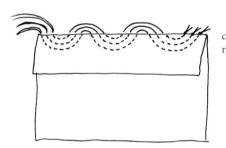

continuous running stitches

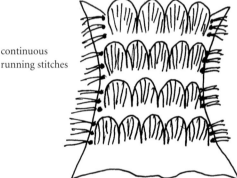

rows of running stitches gathered up and secured

Ideas

A variety of different designs can also be achieved by using different shaped templates, all of which are placed on the fold of the fabric. Right-angle triangles for squares, equilateral triangles for diamond shapes, squares for long rectangles, half-oval (straight edge against fold) for oval shapes, rectangles (long side against fold) for rectangular shapes, and half-hexagon for a whole hexagon after stitching and dyeing – the list is endless!

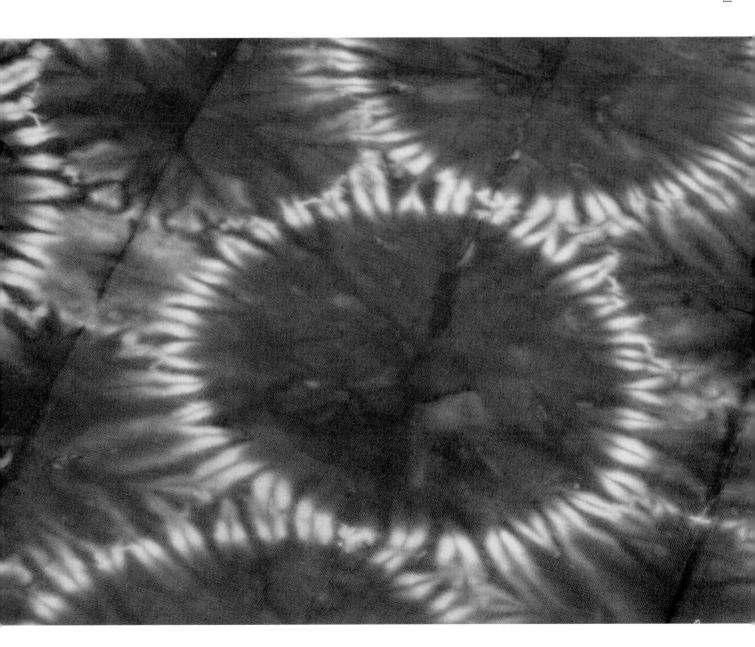

left Patchwork *noren* (door
curtain), showing a variety of
shibori techniques and sashiko
quilting, Japan.

above Large and small circles,
stitched through pleated layers
of cotton lawn cloth, dyed with
Procion MX dye.

Linear designs

Ori-nui shibori (running stitched)

There are a variety of ways to stitch cloth using this technique. Straight lines, running across the cloth, or crossed lines to form a grid are two variations; another is to stitch gently curving lines, *tatewaku* shibori, where the lines can run either diagonally or vertically on the cloth. The fabric is folded along a marked line and running stitches taken close to the fold. The result after dyeing is a double line of white spaces where the dye could not penetrate. If the stitching is done further away from the fold, an intriguing pattern of what I call 'teeth' results and can be quite a talking point!

below Shallow zig-zag lines (detail), stitched on the fold, gathered and dyed in indigo; cotton cloth, Japan.

running stitches
close to the fold

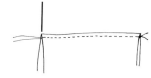

running stitches gathered
tightly and tied off

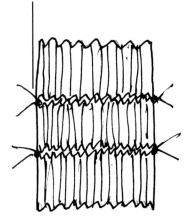

gathered in both directions
to form a grid design

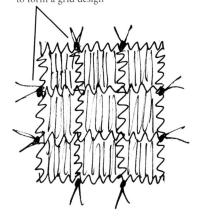

right Diamond lattice shibori,
stitched through pleated layers
of cotton lawn cloth. Dyed
with Procion MX dye.

Technique

1. Take a 40 cm (16 in) square of white cotton fabric and mark or crease a fold line (across the weft) every 5 cm (2 in).
2. Fold the fabric on the first line. Using double thread and beginning with a knot, take running stitches close to the fold line; stitch across to the opposite side of the fabric and leave a thread approximately 8 cm (3 in) long for gathering later.
3. Continue in this way until all the lines of stitch are complete.
4. Pull up the gathers tightly and secure with a reef knot. You may wish to trim some of the long ends of thread off at this stage.
5. Dye fabric using your chosen method. After the dyeing and washing processes, stitches are removed to reveal the *ori-nui* pattern.

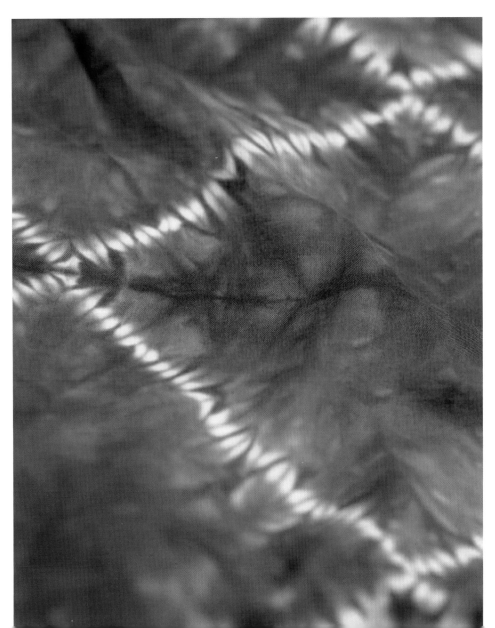

Ideas

- Try this method of stitching using crossed lines. Mark lines in both directions on the cloth. Stitch the horizontal lines first, then the verticals. Gather up all the horizontal lines first, then repeat with the vertical lines (see page 53 for illustration). Dye as before. The resulting design will be a grid-like pattern.

- Another alternative would be to mark the fabric with undulating, flowing lines (see diagram below). For this you will need to make a template or use a flexible curve to mark your lines. Stitch and dye as before.

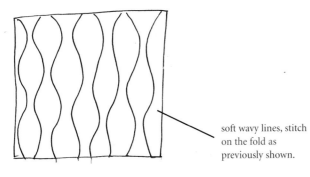

soft wavy lines, stitch on the fold as previously shown.

above Antique African *adire*, stitched on folded cloth through four layers, showing the pale inner layers. Indigo dyed in Nigeria.

right *Reflections XI*, one of a series of quilts using a variety of shibori techniques; stitched resist grid on folded cotton cloth with appliqué, using African adire fabrics, silk and linen. Indigo dyed.

Maki-nui shibori (oversewn stitched)

Similar to *ori-nui* shibori, this technique uses oversewing stitches instead of running stitches to form the pattern left by the resist. Fabric is folded, either singly or double, the stitching, with a double thread, is then taken over the edge of the fold, at a slight diagonal angle. When all the rows of stitching are complete, the thread is then pulled slowly and tightly to form gathers and finished off securely. The resulting designs are rows of chevron-shaped markings, the size of which will depend on how deeply the stitching is taken along the fold. Designs on some of the African clothes that I have in my collection are stitched with fine strands of raffia and are stitched with particularly fine small stitches. The stitching (some of the original stitching is still in place in the fabric), which is very tight, does not appear to have been pulled up into gathers. These designs form grids, star-like shapes, crosses, stripes and borders. These African designs are also often combined with *ne-maki* (tied resist) shibori, either as an infill between other designs or as several rows (eight to nine) to form a border. Try out the *maki-nui* by stitching several rows of differing widths, as well as some African style motifs.

left African *adire alabere* showing some of the raphia stitching still in place; indigo dyed cotton damask from Nigeria.

Technique

1. Take a 40 cm (16 in) square of white cotton fabric and mark or crease a fold line (across the weft) every 5 cm (2 in) on at least half of the cloth. Reserve the rest of the space for some motifs.

2. Using a double thread and starting with a knot, begin oversewing along the edge of the fold. The process can be speeded up by inserting the needle in the fabric and using a scooping motion: take the needle through the fabric from back to front and repeat all the way along. This way you can cover quite a distance before having to pull the thread right through to the front.

3. Carry on in this manner until all the rows have been stitched, remembering that you can vary the thickness of the row of resulting chevrons by taking deeper stitches (just as shallower stitches will result in a narrow row).

4. Stitch some motifs by marking the fabric with a water-soluble pen, then fold on the line and stitch as before.

5. Finally, gather all the rows and motifs carefully and secure the ends of the threads.

6. Dye fabric using your chosen method. After the dyeing and washing process, stitches are removed to reveal the *maki-nui* patterns.

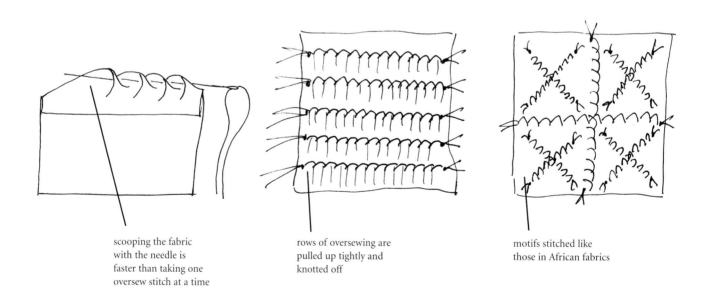

scooping the fabric
with the needle is
faster than taking one
oversew stitch at a time

rows of oversewing are
pulled up tightly and
knotted off

motifs stitched like
those in African fabrics

above Antique *adire oniko* and
alabere indigo dyed cotton
cloth (detail) from Nigeria.

above Antique *adire alabere* and
oniko indigo dyed cotton cloth
(detail) from Nigeria. Note the
softer colour of this cloth, which
is much older than the cloth on
the left.

above *African Odyssey II*. Wall hanging using a combination
of African wax resist prints and adire indigo dyed cotton
cloth. Some of the stitched resist has been sewn on a
machine. Machine pieced and hand and machine quilted.

Maki-age shibori (stitched and tied-resist)

It is possible to combine both the methods of stitched-resist and tied-resist in the same patterns or motifs. The outline of the shape is made by using a running stitch, which is then gathered up tightly and secured. The fabric that is left inside the shape, as a result of the gathering can then be wrapped either with a spiral binding technique or a criss-cross binding technique. The resulting designs have patterning within each motif. Leaves, butterflies and flowers are just a few suggestions for this type of shibori. Experiment with some simple shapes and try both methods of tying to compare the effects. The tying will need to be secured with a single knot.

below Stitched and tied resist; cotton; indigo dyed, China.

Technique

1. Take a 40 cm (16 in) square of white cotton fabric and, using a water-soluble pen, mark (using a template if necessary) some simple leaf shapes on to the fabric.

2. Using a double thread and taking running stitches, follow the line marked around each shape (you could vary this by folding the fabric on the line and stitching very close to the fold). Continue stitching each shape individually.

3. Gather each shape tightly and secure.

4. Now take a length of strong thread and, beginning at the base, make a knot (to secure) close to the gathering stitches, wrap the thread around the puff of excess fabric, easing the folds as you work. The wrapping can be done spirally, tightly from bottom to top and finished with another knot, or alternatively, you could criss-cross bind the fabric. Start in the same way, securing with the knot, then begin wrapping the thread, gradually opening out the spaces up towards the top of the excess fabric; come back down again, crossing the threads as you go. Secure with a single knot.

5. Dye fabric using your chosen method. After the dyeing and washing process, tying and stitches are removed to reveal the pattern within the shapes.

mark leaf shapes on the fabric and stitch around each one using running stitch

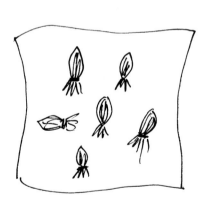

gather up the stitches around each leaf shape and tie off tightly

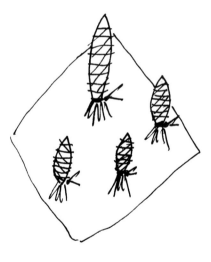

wrap and tie the gathered fabric with a strong thread and tie off tightly at the base

above Stitched and tied resist.
Some of the design has been
stitched on the fold (see
bottom right); cotton, indigo
dyed, China.

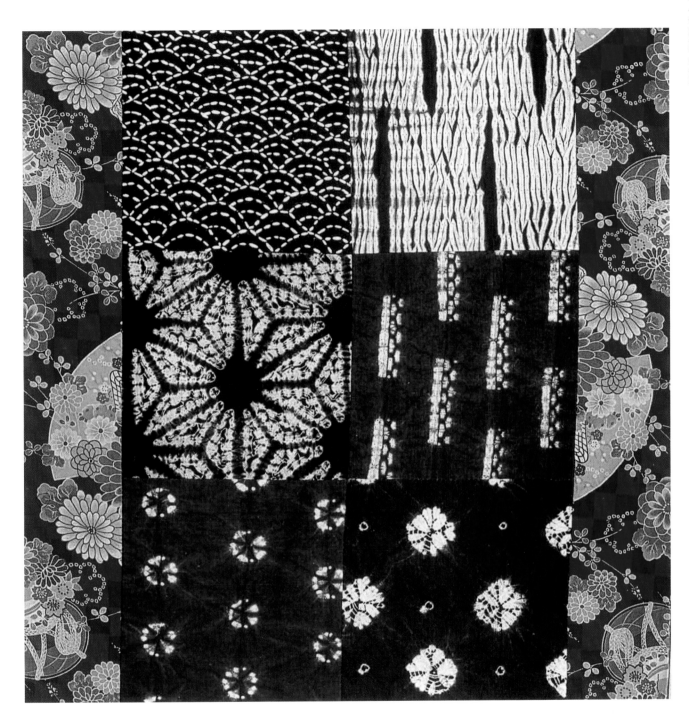

above and left Patchwork *noren* (door curtain). These details show several stitched and stitched and tied shibori techniques, including some sashiko quilting; Japan.

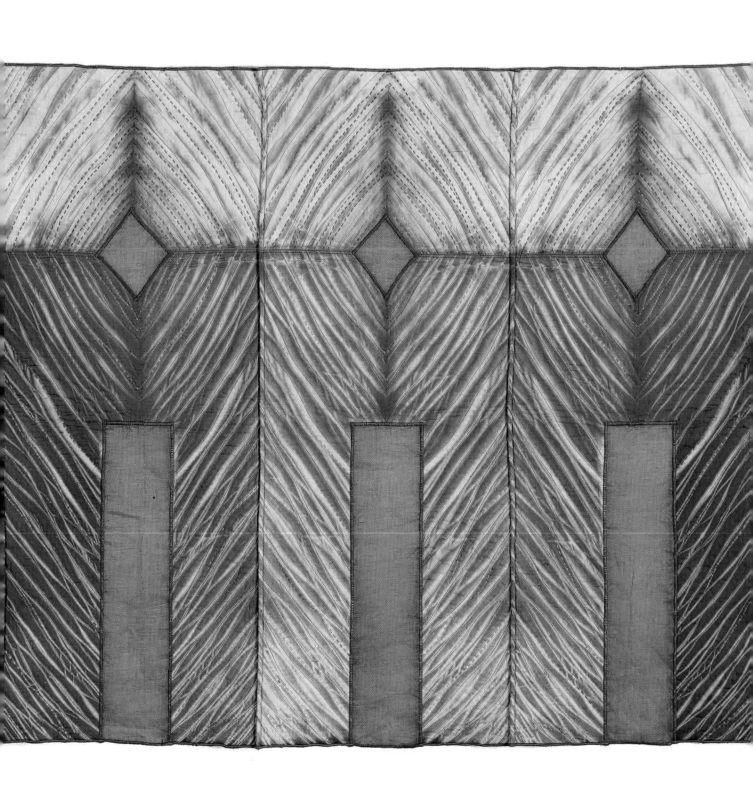

Arashi shibori

Pole-wrapped shibori is known by two names, one is *bomaki*, the other, and probably more famous, is arashi ('storm') shibori. It is this technique that I have been experimenting with since the early 1990s, and is by far my favourite technique. The excitement and element of surprise when a newly dyed piece of fabric is unwrapped never fails to amaze me. It really is a case of you know, but don't know, what you are going to get. No two pieces are ever the same and, as a result, you end up with a unique piece of cloth each time!

Originally the technique in Japan was worked using a long, tapered wooden pole. The fabric was wrapped around this and then wrapped with thread. Every 10 cm (4 in) or so, the fabric was pushed down the pole to form folds. This process continued until all the fabric was wrapped and compressed. The fabric was then lowered into a long narrow vat of indigo dye. The method was to prove time-consuming and costly as two people were required and, as a result, it has been superseded by more cost-effective methods.

left Reflections III (detail). A single piece of cloth was folded in half, concertina pleated and pole wrapped for this wall hanging; Hand and machine quilted, cotton organdie reverse appliqué inserts. Dyed with Procion MX dyes.

above Diagonal *arashi* shibori (left) and horizontal *arashi* shibori (right). Uses Procion MX dyes.

The western way of achieving this fantastic technique is to improvise. The fabric is wrapped around a short length of plastic drainpipe (available from DIY stores or builders' merchants) before being wrapped with a thread; the fabric is pushed into folds to compress it, thereby forming another resist. The pole-wrapped fabric is then immersed, upright, into a dye bath or indigo vat.

above Reflections II. This *arashi* shibori pieced wall hanging uses silk and viscose velvet. It is densely machine quilted following the resist lines of the Procion MX dyeing.

Here are two of the *arashi* techniques that I use, together with some other ideas to try. I hope you have as much fun as I do!

You will need:
- Lightweight white cotton fabric – experiment with this first before moving on to other natural fabrics such as silk, linen, viscose rayon, silk and viscose velvet, and such like
- Strong cotton thread
- Masking tape
- Pole made from plastic drainpipe – one or two pieces approximately 10 cm (4 in) diameter x 50–100 cm (20–40 in) long.

Diagonal stripes: Hosoito ichido kairyō

Technique

1. Cut your fabric into a narrow strip approximately 20 cm (8 in) wide.

2. Begin by wrapping the fabric around the pole in a spiral, taking care not to overlap the fabric. If fabric is wrapped spirally around the pole clockwise, the diagonal design will run from lower left to upper right and vice versa. Secure the ends and the edges (where the fabric meets around the pole) with small pieces of masking tape.

3. Now start wrapping the thread around the fabric on the pole in an anticlockwise direction, taking care to keep an even tension (too tight and you will not be able to compress the fabric). Keeping the thread evenly spaced and straight as you wind will result in even stripes, while crossing the thread and varying the spaces between will result in *matsukaze arashi* ('wind in the pines'). Remove the pieces of masking tape as you go or they will leave another resist on the fabric. Wrap for about 10 cm (4 in). The space between the wraps of thread will determine how wide the folds will be.

4. Stand the pole on a hard surface or hold it against a wall and push the fabric straight down toward the end of the pole, taking care not to let it slip off at the end. Carry on in this way until all the fabric is used up. Secure the thread with a knot or masking tape.

fabric wrapped spirally around a plastic tube and secured with masking tape

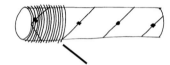

thread wrapped over fabric, clockwise around the tube, keeping an even tension

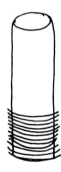

tape removed except for bottom end of tube. Fabric pushed tightly to the bottom end. Make sure thread is secure

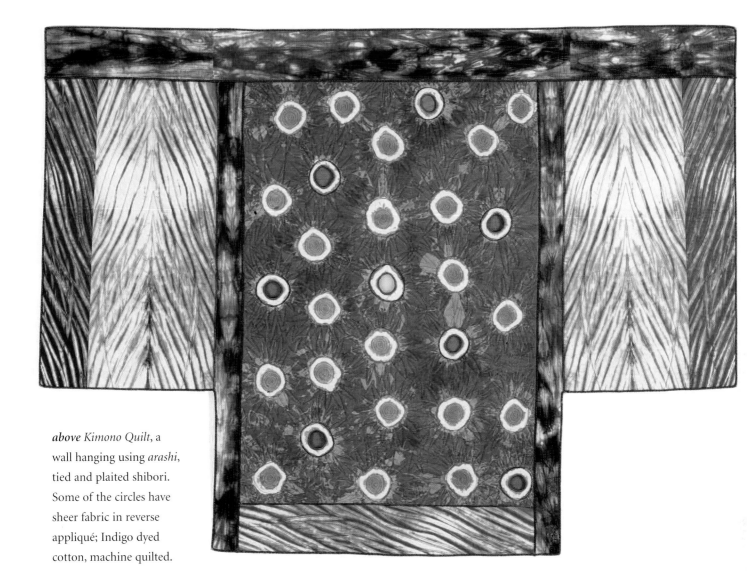

above Kimono Quilt, a wall hanging using *arashi*, tied and plaited shibori. Some of the circles have sheer fabric in reverse appliqué; Indigo dyed cotton, machine quilted.

far left Crosscurrents (detail), a small wall hanging. The fabric was dyed, washed and re-folded then dyed again, resulting in crossed lines; indigo dyed *arashi* shibori using cotton lawn cloth.

left Through a Doorway (detail), a wall hanging using *arashi* shibori, dyed with Procion MX dyes and hand and machine quilted.

5. Depending upon the final finish of the fabric required, you may now wish to soak the fabric in water before dyeing. This will affect the penetration of the dye, making the end result sharper than if dry fabric is immersed in dye. It is particularly important to wet the fabric thoroughly if you intend to dye in indigo. The process will give a more even dye and will prevent bubbles being caught in the folds, and possibly tainting the indigo vat.

6. Dye the fabric, on the pole, using the method of your choice. When rinsing is completed fabric can be removed from the pole by carefully unwinding the thread. (This too will have dyed and I save this to use for quilting.) The resulting piece of patterned fabric can now be washed and dried.

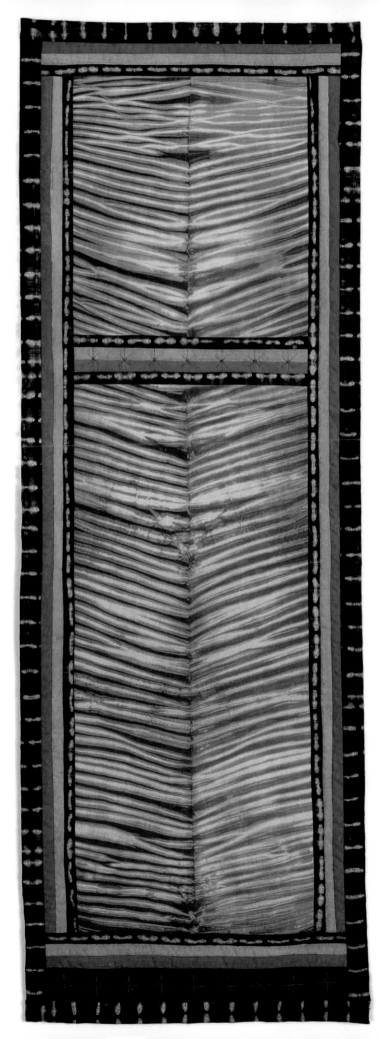

left *Ripples* by Sue Hickman. A combination of hand-dyed indigo cotton and African fabrics work really well in this wall hanging; hand and machine quilting.

right *Shibori Strippy* by Cherry Vernon-Harcourt. Procion MX dyes and Indigo have been used together for the central section of this quilt, based on the traditional North Country 'Strippy' quilt layout; machine quilted.

Ideas

- Try twisting the fabric down the pole as you compress it after wrapping with thread – you will get a design of small diamond-like shapes.
- Fold wider strips of fabric, concertina-style, before wrapping around the pole. This produces a graduated dye effect.
- Wrap several different types of thread around the fabric – this gives a variety of textures to work with when you are quilting or embellishing.
- You can get some interesting effects by wrapping the fabric unevenly or crossing the threads over.
- Leaving the masking tape on during the wrapping process, or placing some on the fabric before you wrap will also give you an interesting result.
- Tie or stitch some of the previous techniques discussed and then pole-wrap the fabric for secondary effect. The options are endless really!

Horizontal stripes: Hosoito yoko kairyō

This version is even easier than the previous one and results in stripes or lines that run
horizontally across the fabric when dyed. The original version wraps the fabric around the
pole; this version involves stitching a tube of fabric. This technique is wonderful for
experimenting (see Ideas on page 76).

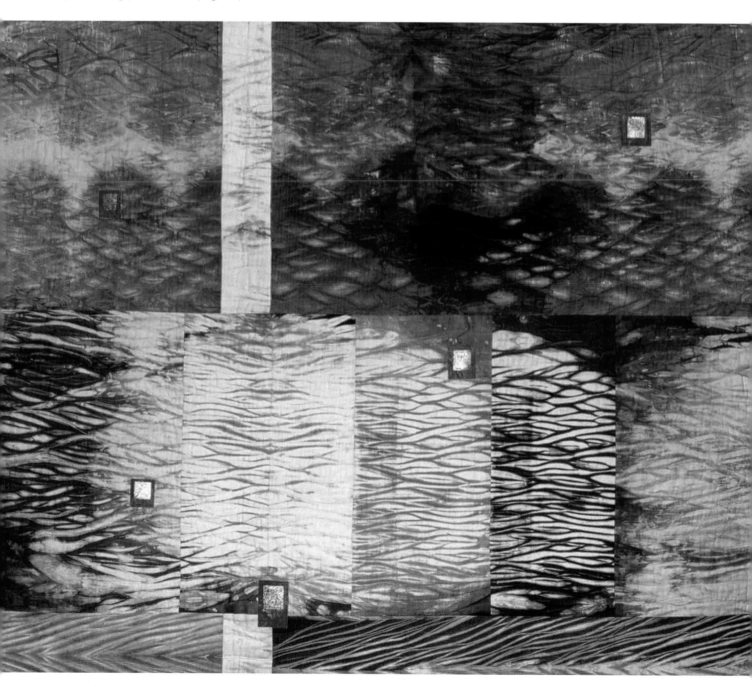

stitch a strip of fabric along its length to form a tube

slide the fabric on to a plastic tube. Push the fabric tightly towards the end of the tube. Thread is not essential if the fabric is a tight fit around the tube.

left Blue Bamboo by Annette Morgan. Taking inspiration from the indigo-dyed fabrics as they 'spoke' to her, Annette has made this striking quilt; cotton fabric, machine pieced and quilted with foiled orange dyed fabric appliqué contrast (photographed by Robert Claxton).

right Homage to Albers by Jan Myers-Newbury. This beautiful quilt uses *arashi* shibori and *itajime* (clamp resist) shibori, with Procion MX dyes, and dyes under-painted; machine pieced and quilted cotton cloth (photographed by Sam Newbury).

Technique

1. Measure the circumference of your pipe. Now cut a strip of fabric that width plus a seam allowance of 1.5 cm (½ in).
2. Stitch the fabric into a long tube along the seam allowance line. Set the sewing machine to the longest stitch (about 5 will do), to ease the removal of the stitches later.
3. Open the tube of fabric at one end and ease it onto the pole. Begin wrapping with thread and push the fabric down as before. Continue in this way until all the fabric is wrapped and compressed on the pipe.
4. Depending upon the final finish of the fabric required, you might want to soak the fabric in water before dyeing. This will affect the penetration of the dye, making the end result sharper than if dry fabric is immersed in dye. It is particularly important to wet the fabric out thoroughly if you intend to dye in indigo. The process will give a more even dye and will prevent bubbles being caught in the folds and possibly tainting the indigo vat.
5. Dye the fabric, on the pole, using the method of your choice. When rinsing is completed, the fabric can be removed from the pole by carefully unwinding the thread. (This too will have dyed and I save this to use for quilting.) The resulting piece of patterned fabric can now be washed and dried.

Ideas

- Try using a wider piece of fabric and stitching tucks into it before joining into a tube; bands of vertical stripes could also be a part of the design.
- If the fabric is a tight enough fit on the pipe, you could omit the wrapping threads and just compress the fabric; this gives a more random strip effect, not unlike the *mokume* ('wood grain') effect shibori.
- Try twisting the fabric as you compress it too – yet another variation!
- I particularly like to experiment with dyeing and then re-wrapping and overdyeing again, sometimes with the same colour, sometimes with a contrast. The effects can be stunning. The list is endless, just let your imagination take over.

left *Birch Eyes* by Jan Myers-Newbury; *arashi* shibori using Procion MX dyes on cotton cloth, machine pieced and quilted (photographed by Sam Newbury).

left *Agape* by Jan Myers-Newbury; *arashi* shibori in a myriad of colours, using Procion MX dyes on cotton cloth. Machine pieced and quilted (Photographed by Sam Newbury).

left *Cats Game II* by Jan Myers-Newbury, a quilt using *arashi* and *itajime* (clamp resist) shibori; Procion MX dyes on cotton, machine pieced and quilted (photographed by Sam Newbury).

Itajime – folded and bound/clamp-resist

The process of folding fabric and then clamping it between boards or sticks is thought to have originated in the 8th century, but with the emergence of chemical dyes in the 19th century, the technique began to flourish. These dyes produce wonderful subtle effects, which are not so possible with indigo (although I have had some limited success with this). Katanō Suzuki, who invented the *arashi* shibori has been credited with developing the technique at Arimatsu, where the technique is known as *kekka* shibori.

The fabric is folded into wide vertical pleats, subsequently folded into squares, rectangles or triangles, and then clamped between two pieces of wood or similar material (these should have little notches cut into them for the binding thread to rest in). The shapes of the boards will determine the resulting pattern on the dyed fabric. The bundle of fabric is then bound with a strong thread or a clamping device. The pressure exerted during the binding or clamping process will affect how the dye penetrates the fabric.

You will need:
* Lightweight white cotton fabric – experiment with this first before moving onto other natural fabrics such as silk, linen, viscose rayon, silk and viscose velvet, and such like
* Strong cotton thread or G clamps (or similar)
* Boards – shaped pieces of wood or similar material cut to fit the final width of pleated fabric

left Antique *kekka itajime* (clamp resist) shibori on cotton cloth, Japan.

Naname Gōshi ('lattice')

The pattern that the dye leaves behind using this technique is a form of lattice – the triangular shapes are revealed with a combination of both strong dark and light areas.

Technique

1. Take a 40 cm (16 in) square of white cotton fabric and dampen well. Lay the fabric flat on a work surface and accordion pleat the fabric into wide, even vertical pleats.

2. Take the corner of the pleated fabric and make a diagonal fold by aligning the right-hand edge with the top edge of the fabric (A), forming a triangle; now turn the fabric over and fold back and forth, still keeping the triangle shape (B). When folding is finished (C), place a triangular-shaped piece of wood on either side of the bundle of fabric and tie or clamp it into place (D).

3. Dyeing with Procion MX fibre-reactive dye is the preferred technique to use when dyeing *itajime*. The folded and clamped fabric is dipped into the dye, one side of the triangle at a time. The same colour can be used throughout, or different colours can be used on each side. I have also successfully dyed similar patterns by immersing the whole bundle of fabric into a bucket of dye.

4. When the dyeing is complete, remove the bindings or clamps and open the fabric out very carefully – allow it to dry flat or on a washing line to protect the dye from bleeding further and smudging or destroying the design.

5. Complete the process with a final wash and dry.

A

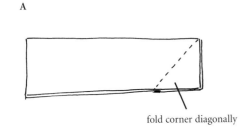

fold corner diagonally

B

fold back and forth until whole length is complete
and you are left with a triangular pad of fabric

C

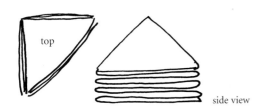

top

side view

D

ties

wooden clamp at
either end

left Itajime (clamp resist) shibori using cottons, indigo and Procion MX dyes. Plastic clothes pegs and bag clips were used on folded cloth.

left Lattice *itajime* using cotton cloth and Procion MX dyes. The cloth was folded and clamped, and dye was trickled down the folded edges.

left Swazi Stars by Barbara Corbett shows shapes made by clamping plastic stars either side of folded cloth; indigo dyed, machine pieced and quilted.

right Coronae by Jan Myers-Newbury. This glowing quilt uses *arashi* shibori and *itajime* (clamp resist) shibori on dyed cotton cloth using Procion MX dyes. The dyes are also under painted. Machine pieced and quilted (photography by Sam Newbury).

above and left Shibori Sampler (left) and close-up detail (above). In this quilt I have used a variety of techniques. Stars form the border, using *itajime* (clamp resist) shibori; Indigo dyed cottons, machine pieced and quilted.

Ideas

- Try folding the fabric into squares, rectangles or equilateral triangles and then binding or clamping to create other patterns.
- Use a variety of shapes to clamp on to the bundle of fabric – try circles, squares, sticks, stars (the children's large 'glow in the dark' stars work very well).
- Try clamping with spring clamps or G clamps, but remember that any fabric that becomes scrunched will also resist. I find everyday items such as plastic-backed clips, clothes pegs, bulldog and paper clips, as well as rubber bands, all produce some interesting effects.
- Try space dyeing some of the fabrics resisted and dyed in this way too. The effects can be quite amazing.
- This is a wonderful technique when used on sheer fabrics such as silk organza and georgette, fine *habotai* (for scarves) and cotton organdie. Fabrics can be layered, stitched and then cut back to reveal different textures.

Tesuji shibori – pleated and bound

Pleated and bound fabric will produce both vertical and horizontal stripes, and is especially interesting if several colours of dye are used. The fabric can be bound along the entire length or at intervals, sometimes bound on to a core of thick rope. The technique has been used for many years and is still popular today. The Gambia, in West Africa, produces some wonderful dyed fabrics using this simple technique with both fibre-reactive and natural dyes. The use of indigo and kola nut (*gara*, which originated in Sierra Leone) produces a fascinating combination of shades of blue and brown.

One design created by tying the pleated fabric to a core of rope, *yanagi* ('willow') shibori, results in a pattern that represents the weeping branches of the willow tree. The fabric is first tied with random *kumo* shibori (see Chapter 2). It is then pleated and wrapped around a rope, where it is tied again before being immersed in the dye. Shibori artist Hiroshi Murase from Arimatsu gave instruction on this specific technique during his visit to the UK recently, and I had the great fortune to attend the session and so learn the technique.

left Yanagi ('willow') shibori; indigo dyed cotton *yukata* cloth by Ken-ichi Utsuki at his studio, Aizenkobo, Kyoto, Japan.

You will need:
- Experiment with lightweight white cotton fabric first before moving onto other natural fabrics such as silk, linen, viscose rayon, silk and viscose velvet, and such like
- Strong soft cotton thread and fine ordinary cotton thread
- Nylon rope – optional for core wrapped shibori

Tesuji shibori

Technique

1. Take a 40 cm (16 in) square of white cotton fabric and dampen well. Lay the fabric flat on a work surface and accordion pleat the fabric into narrow, even vertical pleats (A).

2. Loosely wrap the pleats with some of the fine thread to keep them in place while working (B).

3. Now begin to bind the pleats, evenly spaced, with the stronger thread (C). In order to keep an even tension, the fabric can be clamped on to the edge of the work surface or a special stand can be made from a thick stick, usually bamboo, with a V-shaped notch cut into it (*tesugi dai*). The binding process is called *tatsumaki*.

4. Dampen the fabric again if it has started to dry, and dye using the technique of your choice.

5. After dyeing, remove the binding and open up the fabric carefully; wash and dry the fabric in the usual way.

right I couldn't resist buying this pleated resist space-dyed cotton cloth for future use in a quilt! By Leslie Morgan, using Procion MX dyes.

Ideas

- Try pleating the fabric and tying at intervals – the stripes will alternate with wider bands of solid colour.

- Wrap the pleated fabric around a core of nylon rope at the beginning of step 3 for a more pronounced effect in the stripes.

- Try sticking masking tape on the fabric before pleating to void areas for another resist.

- Pleat and dye, then repeat the process by re-pleating the fabric, either vertically again or horizontally, as desired.

- Pleat the fabric and bind loosely with fine thread; lay into a shallow tray and space dye the fabric. If you use a longer piece of fabric, try scrunching up the ends a little to give interesting border effects.

A

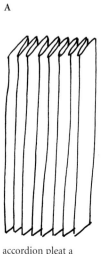

accordion pleat a
length of fabric

B

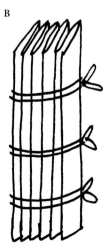

bind loosely

C

bind tightly keeping
an even tension

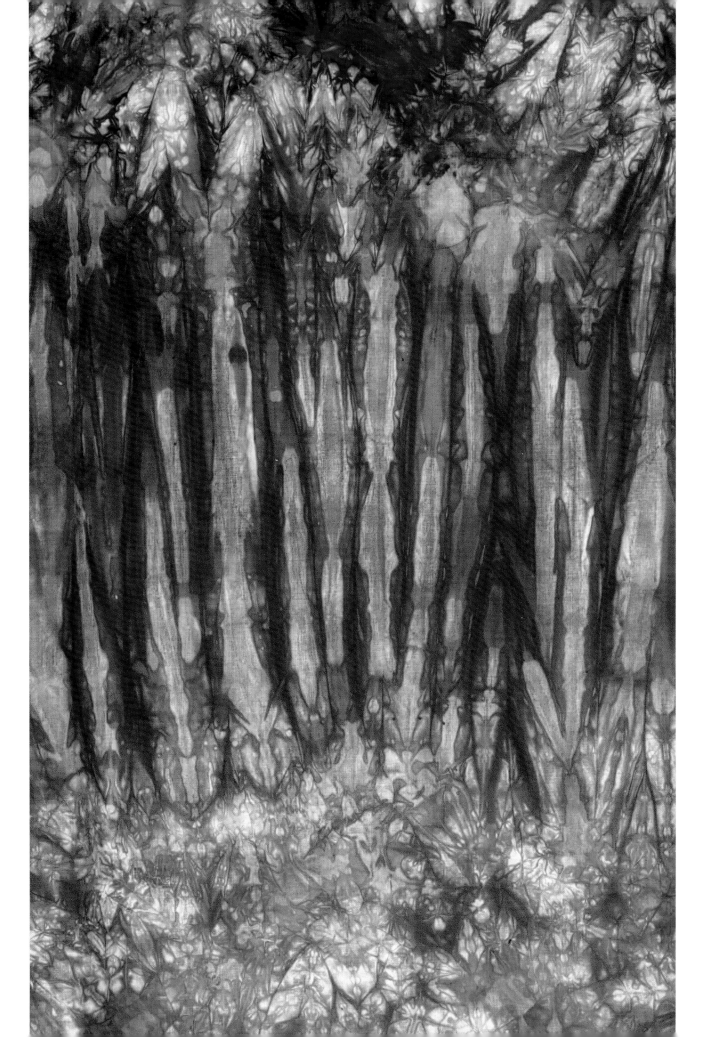

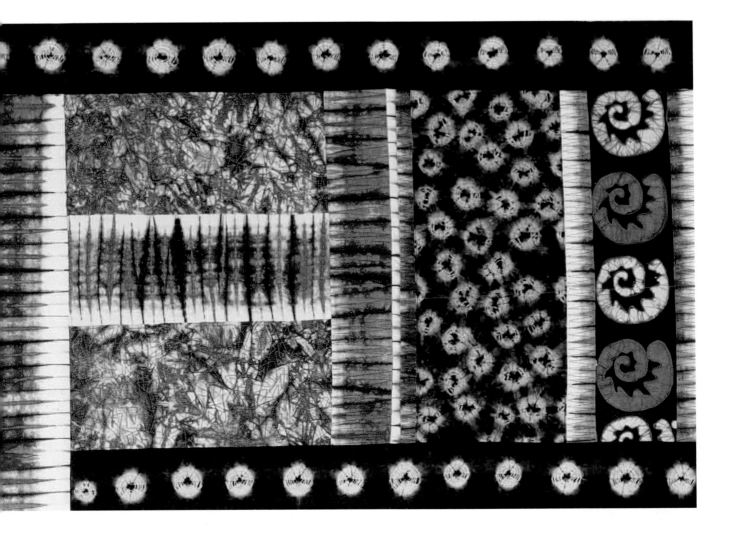

above *African Odyssey III* (detail) shows the pleated and bound indigo and kola nut dyed fabric; and hand machine quilted.

above right Pleated and bound linen cloth using indigo dye.

below right Pleated and bound cotton cloth, space dyed using Procion MX dyes.

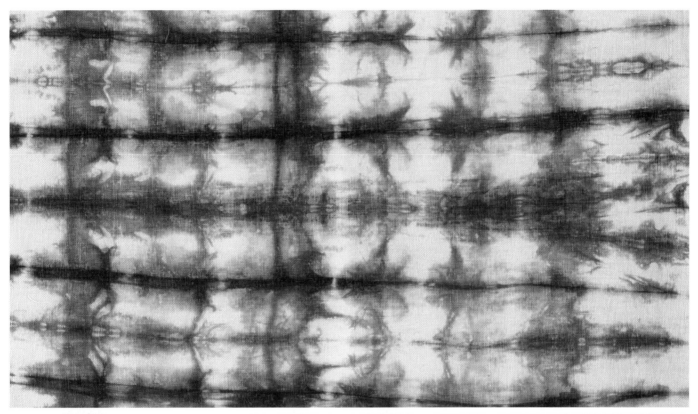

Yanagi shibori ('willow')

This is the wonderful design that Hiroshi Murase taught at the Knitting and Stitching Show in Harrogate, North Yorkshire in 2005. The whole class had a wonderful time, sitting in a huge circle, with our backs to each other, acting as weights on the chairs while we bound the pre-dyed silk scarf we had been given. To improvise, as we did not have a *yokobiki dai* (tying stand), we were given a long bent hook (very sharp) attached to a piece of string. This was tied, hook down to the chair in front of us, and we marked dots on the scarf (with a water-soluble pen) for the first process, the *kumo* ('spider web') tying. The scarf was hooked on at the dot and Mr Murase showed us how to wrap the thread, keeping the scarf as taut as possible (the tension was achieved by pulling on the fabric as it was hooked). When the *kumo* were completed, the scarf was then removed from the hook and pleated. The second stage of wrapping around the rope core began. A loop of string was given to everyone and we tied this to the chair in front (having removed the hook); a second loop was made in this and the pleated scarf and rope core were threaded into this and the loop pulled tight. This was our improvised *tesuji dai!*

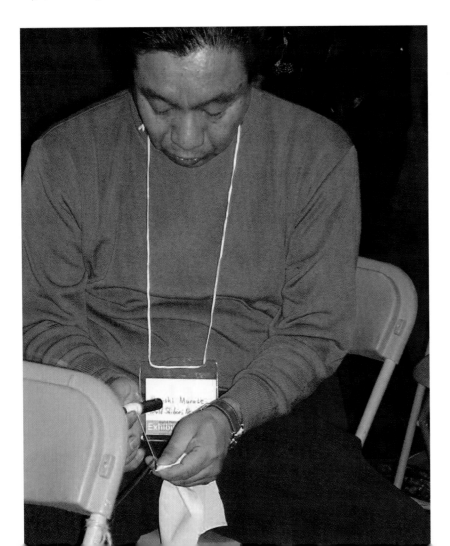

left Japanese shibori artist, Hiroshi Murase demonstrates tying the *yanagi* ('willow') shibori technique at the class I attended (photograph by Janice Gunner).

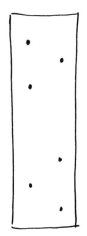

A

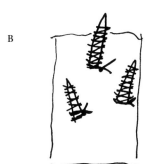

B

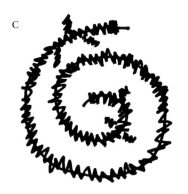

C

Mr Murase then went on to show us how to wrap the scarf. The thread was held on a stick and passed under and over the scarf and rope, and wrapped as evenly as we could. We left the *kumo*-wrapped areas free, while holding the scarf as taut as possible. Every 10 cm (4 in), the scarf was loosened in the loop and the rope of fabric was moved up, tightened again and the wrapping continued until the whole length of the scarf was complete. The scarf was then removed, soaked in water and eventually dyed in acid dye for a short time. Our scarves were returned to us on the rope core, taken home and washed and then untied and removed from the rope.

Technique

1. Take a 30 x 120 cm (12 x 47 in) length of fine cotton or silk *habotai* fabric (or a ready-prepared silk scarf of a similar size). Dye this first if you wish the background to be a colour other than white.

2. Mark dots on the fabric (three randomly spaced on each end to start) with a water-soluble pen (A). Wrap each *kumo* by pinching the dot and, starting with a knot, wrap the pinched fabric from bottom to top and back again. Secure with a knot (B).

3. Pleat the fabric (or scarf) in your left hand (vice versa if you are left-handed) and place the rope against the back of the pleating. Improvise if necessary by securing the rope and pleating together with a rubber band to start with. Clamp to the edge of the work surface and begin wrapping with a strong thread (D). Wrap evenly, keeping the tension constant and avoid wrapping in the *kumo*. Continue until wrapping is complete.

4. Soak the fabric, which will probably have coiled up at this stage (C), in water for 15 minutes.

5. Now dye using your chosen technique. If you are using Procion MX, fix the silk (if used) with some distilled white vinegar instead of soda ash.

6. After dyeing is complete, rinse, wash, and remove both the ties and the fabric from the rope. The fabric will be wonderfully textured with pleats at this stage. They will not, however, remain in the fabric permanently but, if you allow the fabric to dry naturally, you can appreciate them while they last. You will still end up with a beautiful piece of fabric – it will just be flat and patterned!

D

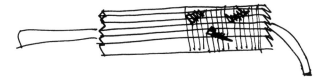

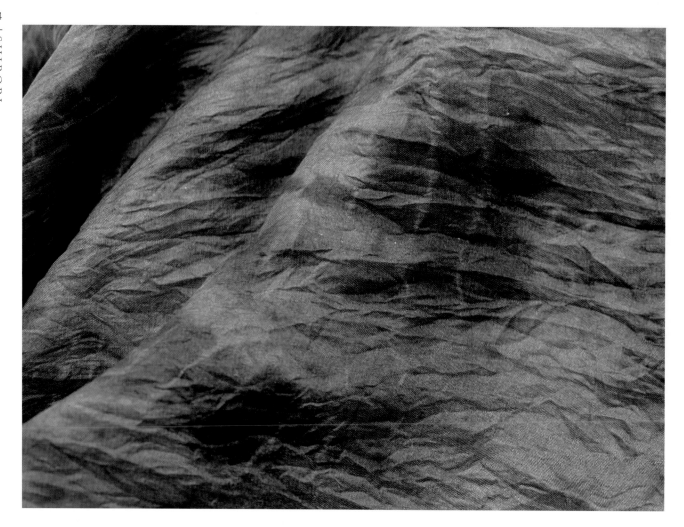

above My *yanagi* shibori scarf; silk, dyed using acid dyes during the Hiroshi Murase workshop (photograph by Janice Gunner).

right Pleated and bound *tesuji* shibori by Hiroshi Murase, Arimatsu, Japan. The horizontal stripes show where the thread bound the pleated cloth (photograph by Janice Gunner).

left *Reflecting the Blues* by
Margaret Starr; hand quilting
on pleated and bound shibori.
Indigo dyed cotton cloth was
used for this long, narrow wall
hanging.

above Indigo dyed shibori
using the crackle and plaited
techniques described earlier.

right Procion MX dyes used
for the techniques described.

Dyeing techniques

This chapter sets out some of the techniques that I use to dye my prepared shibori fabrics. These are not set in stone, and you may already have previous experience of dyeing and wish to use your own methods, but they all work for me. The quantities in the recipes will dye approximately 2 m (6½ ft) of fabric.

As with all dyeing techniques, there are some very important, specific health and safety rules to adhere to, not only for your own safety, but also for those around you when you are working, so read the following carefully.

Dyes and their auxiliaries (soda ash, washing soda, urea, caustic soda and Hydrotherm DD) are chemicals and, as such, should be treated with care and respect. Each of the techniques that I will be explaining to you – immersion dyeing, space dyeing (both with Procion MX dyes) and indigo – will include the safety procedures for you to follow.

All dyeing equipment should be kept separate from your usual household utensils. Please make sure that you read the instructions carefully, but most of all, have fun.

Immersion, space and indigo dying

Not all of these items will be used for every technique; they are, however, a good basic kit.
Each recipe will mention the particular items needed.

You will need:

- 1 standard-size household bucket
- 1 shallow plastic tray (I use a cat litter tray)
- 1 large measuring jug – 2 litre (3¼ pint) capacity with millilitre and fluid ounce markings
- 1 small measuring jug – 1 litre (1¾ pint) capacity with millilitre and fluid ounce markings
- A stick to stir-dye bath
- Small disposable spoons for mixing dyes and soda ash
- Set of measuring spoons: tablespoon (15 ml), dessertspoon (10 ml), teaspoon (5 ml) and ½ teaspoon (2.5 ml) – either metal or plastic
- Small plastic medicine measure 25 ml (1 fl oz) or 50 ml (2 fl oz)
- Plastic pipettes
- 3 clean empty jam jars with lids
- 2 clean empty fabric softener bottles with side handle, 2 litre (3¼ pint) capacity
- Protective clothing – face mask, safety spectacles, rubber gloves, PVC apron or lab coat, and wear old clothes and shoes
- Protective covers for work surfaces (medium-weight plastic)
- Kitchen paper towels
- Cooking salt
- Soda ash or washing soda
- Urea
- Procion MX dye in the colour of your choice. If you wish to use a blue, I suggest either indigo navy (Kemtex) or navy (Jacquard)
- Caustic soda
- Hydrotherm DD (Hydros)
- Synthetic indigo vat 60% grains

Using the spoons for measuring is easier and safer than having to weigh very small amounts, therefore all measurements are given as the spoon size or its volume.

Health and safety for immersion and space dyeing

Dyes can produce allergic reactions, especially to the respiratory tract. Always follow the advice given here.

- Procion MX dyes are chemicals, please treat them with respect. Decant and clearly label urea, washing soda and soda ash as they are all white powders they are easily mistaken for each other.
- Clear all work surfaces and cover with protective plastic sheeting.
- Always wear protective clothing and a face mask while the dyes are being dispensed and mixed. Make sure the area is well ventilated.
- Never eat, drink or smoke while working with dyes or dyeing processes.
- Store dyes and auxiliaries (urea, washing soda and soda ash) in a cool, dry place and away from children and pets.
- Clean up any spillages immediately and use soap and water to remove dye if splashed on the skin. Stubborn stains can be removed by using Reduran, a proprietary skin cleaner.
- Dispose of the exhausted dye bath normally with plenty of cold running water.

right Twice-dyed *arashi* shibori by Jacqui Veasey, using orange and blackcurrant Procion MX dyes (photograph by Janice Gunner).

Immersion dyeing

Recipe

- 4 tbsp (60 ml) cooking salt
- 4–6 tsp (20–30 ml) dye powder
- 4 tbsp (60 ml) urea
- 2 tbsp (30 ml) soda ash or 4 tbsp (60 ml) washing soda
- Synthrapol/Metapex 38/Colsperse (This is a detergent for use with Procion MX dyes – it is excellent for cleaning the fabric before dyeing and also for rinsing after dyeing)

Technique

1. Measure the cooking salt into a bucket containing 2 litres (3½ pints) hot water; stir to dissolve and add 2 litres (3½ pints) cold water.
2. Dissolve the 4–6 tsp (20–30 ml) of dye powder in a small measuring jug with a little warm water and stir into a paste.
3. Dissolve urea in ½ litre (1 pint) hot water, and top up with ½ litre (1 pint) cold water. Stir into the dye paste and add to the bucket, stirring to mix into the salt solution.
4. Immerse your prepared fabric into the dye bucket; stir and leave for 15 minutes.
5. Dissolve soda ash (or washing soda) in 1 litre (1¾ pints) hot water. Move the fabrics to the side of the dye bucket and pour in the soda solution. Continue dyeing for another hour, stirring occasionally to give an even colour.
6. Empty the dye bucket into the sink and rinse your fabric under cold running water until it runs clear.
7. Remove the clamps, ties, stitching and poles and soak fabrics in ½ tsp (2.5 ml) Synthrapol/Metapex 38/Colsperse solution, dissolved in warm to hot water, around 60 °C (140°F), for 20 minutes. Rinse the fabric again until the water is clear. Dry the fabric, iron it and stand back and admire!

right Cotton cloths of various weights using Procion MX dyes for *arashi*, *itajime* and stitched resist shibori.

Space dyeing

Space dyeing is a great way to experiment with a variety of colours in one dyeing session. The colours are left to mix in the tray, with little or no movement, allowing some spectacular colour combinations to evolve. The method given here is one I have formulated over many years of experimenting and it always gives me good results. My only important bit of advice here is: don't be tempted to poke the fabric about too much, you could end up with a colour that resembles mud!

Recipe

- 4 tbsp (60 ml) salt
- 2 tbsp (30 ml) soda ash or 4 tbsp (60 ml) washing soda
- 3 tsp (15 ml) urea
- 3 tsp (15 ml) dye; 1 each of 3 different colours

Technique

First make up salt and soda solutions as follows:

1. Dissolve salt in 1 litre (1¾ pints) of very hot water; stir to dissolve and decant into one of the clean empty fabric softener bottles. Top the bottle up with cold water and leave the lid off until tepid. Label the bottle 'Salt solution'.

2. Dissolve the soda ash in 1 litre (1¾ pints) of very hot water; stir to dissolve and decant into the other clean empty fabric softener bottle. Top the bottle up with cold water and leave the lid off until tepid. Label the bottle 'Soda solution'.

These solutions will keep indefinitely, providing the cap is screwed on tightly. Store in a cool place. If the salt or soda has crystallized when you next use it, stand the bottles with their lids off in the sink filled with very hot water for about 15 minutes. Replace the lids and shake well to dissolve the crystals.

3. Dampen your fabric and place into a cat litter tray. Threads can also be dampened and added – you will then have some matching threads (I usually lay them on top of the fabrics) to stitch with.

4. Take the three jam jars and place 1 tsp (5 ml) urea in each one. Measure 1 tsp (5 ml) dye powder A and add to one jar; repeat this process with dye B into the second jar and dye C into the third jar.

5. Dissolve the urea and dye in each jar with 12 ml (½ fl oz) of the salt solution, to make a paste. Measure 50 ml (2 fl oz) salt solution into each jar and stir well. When you are ready to begin dyeing, add 50 ml (2 fl oz) of soda solution to each jar and stir again.

6. If the dye has still not dissolved, screw the lid on the jar and shake well over the sink. Be careful: the jar may leak, so remove the lid carefully over the sink.

7. Spoon half of the jar contents with dye A into spaces on the fabrics in the tray. Use a pipette to carefully squirt the dye solution into folds and gathers. Repeat with dyes B and C.

8. Take out the threads if you have included some and place these on some kitchen paper on the work surface. Carefully turn the fabrics over, rearranging them as necessary and return the threads if wished (I sometimes replace the threads in the dye solution if a darker colour is required).

9. Repeat step 7 until all the dye is used up. Remove the threads and leave in a shallow tray to absorb the colour.

10. Leave the fabrics for a minimum of 1 hour. I have left fabrics overnight sometimes if darker colours are required.

11. Rinse the fabrics until the water runs clear. Remove clamps, ties, stitching and poles and soak fabrics in ½ tsp (2.5 ml) Synthrapol/Metapex 38/Colsperse solution, dissolved in warm to hot water, around 60 °C (140 °F), for 20 minutes. Rinse the fabric again until the water is clear. Dry fabric, iron it and stand back and admire!

below Tesuji (pleated and bound) and *itajime* (clamp resist) space dyed shibori; cotton cloth and Procion MX dyes.

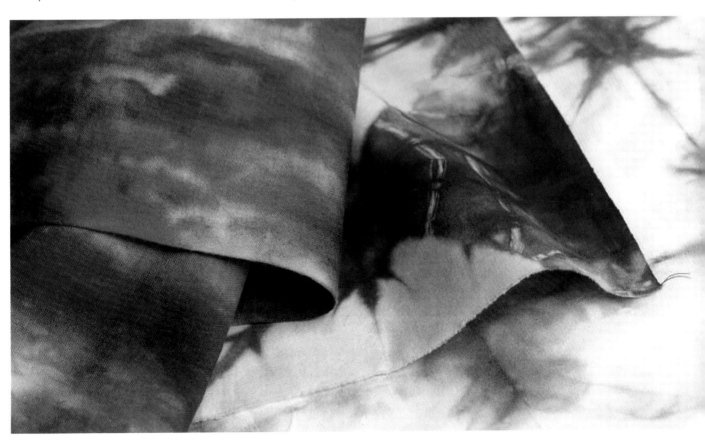

above Indigo dyed *tesuji* and
tied resist shibori on cotton
cloth (photograph by Janice
Gunner).

right *Ripples II* (detail) by Sue
Hickman shows the *arashi*
shibori technique with
machine and hand quilting
using contrast thread.

Indigo dyeing

If you have never dyed with indigo before, you are in for a treat. It really is the most magical of all the dyeing techniques. You start off with a vat or bucket of not very pleasant smelling, yellowy green liquid. Dip in your fabrics, pull them out slowly and away from the bucket. The greenish coloured fabric then magically turns blue before your very eyes. You let it oxidize and then return it to the vat, where it turns green again, repeat the process and it turns a slightly darker shade of blue – you can keep doing this until you have achieved the depth of colour required.

There are many books with recipes for indigo dyeing; they all vary, so have a go at the method I have explained here, which is adapted from a workshop that I attended with Delia Copland, and then experiment with some of the other methods.

Health and safety for indigo dyeing

- Clear all work surfaces and cover with protective plastic sheeting.
- Always wear protective clothing, rubber gloves, a face mask and safety spectacles while the caustic soda, Hydrotherm DD (Hydros) and indigo are being dispensed and mixed. Make sure the area is well ventilated.
- Never eat, drink or smoke while working with dyes or dyeing processes.
- Store dyes and auxiliaries – caustic soda, Hydrotherm DD (Hydros), washing soda and soda ash) – clearly labelled, in a cool, dry place and away from children and pets.
- Caustic soda will burn if splashed on to the skin; if this occurs, rinse the affected area with cold running water and seek medical attention.
- Clean up any spillages immediately, and clean utensils and the sink as soon as you have finished with them.

Dyes can produce allergic reactions, especially to the respiratory tract. Always follow the advice given here.

right A selection of cloths, some prepared for dyeing (using stitched and tied techniques), others already dyed in indigo by master dyer Ken-ichi Utsuki, Kyoto, Japan (photograph by Janice Gunner).

Recipe

- 5 litres (8¾ pints) water
- 2 tbsp (30 ml) salt
- 1 tbsp (15 ml) caustic soda, or 4 tbsp (60 ml) washing soda, which is safer
- 2 tsp (10 ml) Hydrotherm DD (Hydros)
- 2 tbsp (20 ml) Indigo vat 60% grains

Technique

1. Dissolve the salt in 1 litre (1¾ pints) of hot water and top up to 5 litres (8¾ pints) with warm water in a bucket (preferably without ridges around the inside and bottom).
2. Slowly sprinkle the caustic soda in and stir to dissolve (use washing soda with silk).

Never pour water on to caustic soda – it will boil up and is dangerous. Always wear a mask, safety spectacles and rubber gloves and use in a well-ventilated room.

3. Sprinkle in the Hydrotherm DD (Hydros) and stir to dissolve.
4. Slowly sprinkle in the Indigo vat 60% grains into the bucket and stir gently to fully disperse.
5. Cover the bucket with cling film, lowering it carefully, right down to the surface of the bucket. Exclude as much air as possible and leave the contents to rest for at least 1 hour before using.
6. After 1 hour, remove the cling film, taking care to collect any scum that has formed. The surface will turn slightly blue from the reaction with oxygen.
7. Carefully and slowly immerse the prepared fabrics into the bucket. Be careful to make sure that the fabrics are damp before you put them in, otherwise the air inside dry fabrics will upset the balance in the bucket.
8. Leave for 2 minutes and then slowly remove the fabrics, taking care not to let the dripping fabrics introduce air bubbles into the vat.
9. Oxidize (lift up into the air and move folds, gathers etc. to allow oxidization to take place in the lower layers) for 5 minutes. Hang on a line outside or spread out on the ground if possible to allow this to take place fully.
10. Return the fabrics to the bucket for 2 minutes as before and remove to oxidize for 5 minutes. Repeat this stage until your fabric is the depth of colour required. Carry on using the bucket until the indigo is exhausted.
11. Dispose of the contents carefully by flushing the liquid away with plenty of cold water to dilute it.
12. Hang or spread the fabrics out for the final oxidization and leave to dry if possible.
13. Rinse fabrics well and remove ties, stitches, clamps etc. Some oxidization may still take place at this stage. Wash the fabrics, rinse, dry and iron. Stand back and marvel at the amazing array of fabrics ready to use in your work.

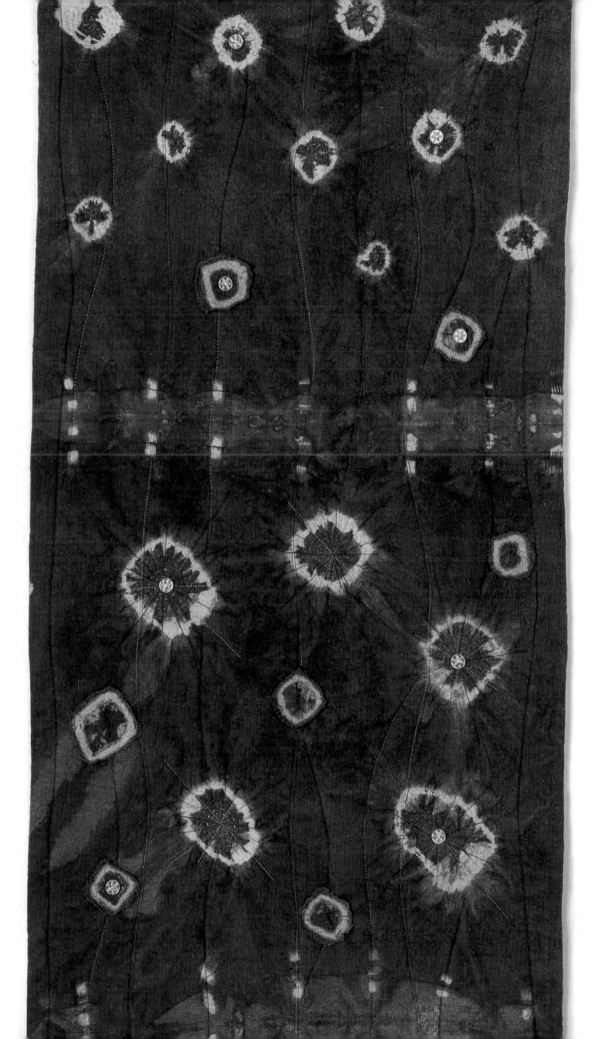

Below and left Indigo Garden
by Joan Randall shows tied
resist using different sizes of
circles and clamp resist using
clothes pegs; whole cloth quilt,
machine and hand quilted and
embellished with buttons.
Indigo dyed silk noil cloth.

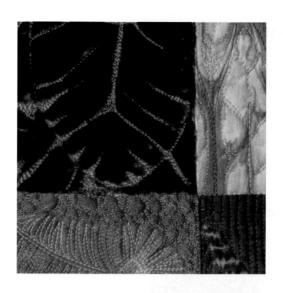

right and below Featherbed
Blues by Claire Higgott. This
little quilt shows a variety of
shibori techniques using
indigo dye; machine pieced,
machine and hand quilted
with some appliqué.

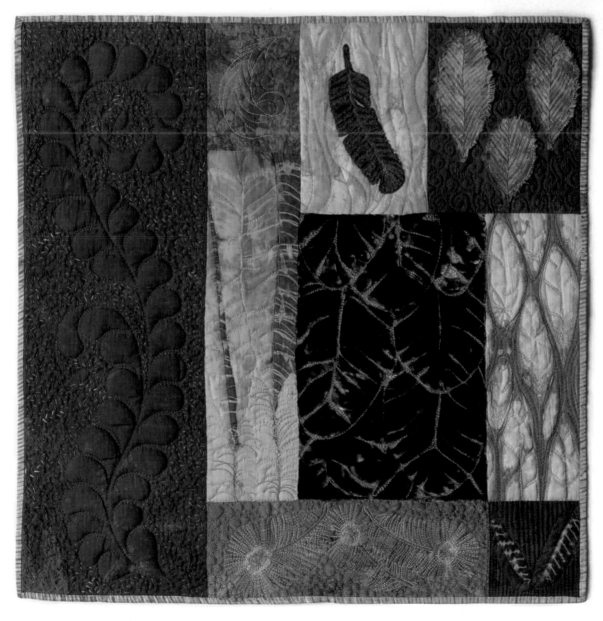

above *Indigo Dyeing in the Barn* by Alex Rankin was made as a result of
an indigo dyeing workshop I taught at Alex's farm. She has combined
the shibori with a patchwork technique I devised called 'curves in the
cabin'; cotton, silk and velvet cloths, machine pieced and hand quilted.

Shibori sampler wall hanging

Now that you have experimented with some of the shibori and dyeing techniques in this book, I can't leave you with all that fabric just sitting there. Yes, I know you think it is so precious that you never want to cut it up, but that will never do. Be brave, cut it up and make yourself (or a friend or relative for that matter) something to hang on a wall to remind yourself (or them) how clever you are!

I'm not going to give you specific sizes and step-by-step instructions on how to make a clone of one of my pieces. I want you to use a design wall and let the fabric speak to you, for your finished piece to be your own unique record of your shibori explorations.

left *Shibori Sampler* uses a variety of techniques, designed by placing fabrics on a wall and moving the pieces around until I was happy; machine pieced, machine quilted and couched threads.

right *Surface Tension I*. Made as part of a challenge for the exhibition '4 x 4', and includes fabric supplied by Annette Claxton, Jennifer Hollingdale and Grit Traum. I have combined my own indigo dyed *arashi* shibori with African fabrics, polyester sheer, and cotton dress fabric; machine pieced and densely machine quilted.

Technique

1. Collect together all the fabrics you have dyed. Sort them into large, medium and small designs and include some plain or contrasting fabrics if you wish.

2. Take a crib-sized (or larger) piece of cotton wadding (batting) – I prefer Hobbs Heirloom (80% cotton and 20% polyester) – and stick it to a wall with masking tape, or use a proper design wall if you are lucky enough to have one.

3. Pick out your best piece of fabric and place it on the design wall, anywhere to start with; if you are confused, try the top left-hand corner.

4. Look at the other fabrics and try some of them next to the best one. Fold the fabrics smaller if necessary; cut some narrow strips of plain or contrast fabric and look for motifs that you could isolate. Creative cutting is what I call it!

5. Remember to keep standing away from your design: squint or look through a camera lens or reducing glass (or binoculars round the wrong way) to see if it looks OK. Decide whether you want a balanced symmetrical design, or a more risky asymmetric look. Think about repetition of motifs; work with odd numbers if you do this, or use the rule of thirds – it is more pleasing to the eye. Don't make the focal point right in the middle – the eye is drawn there and the surrounding areas get lost. Plan your design so that it takes the viewer's eyes around the whole work, but remember to drop in some specific areas of interest – small accents – so that they have to get closer to the work to see them.

6. Decide whether it needs borders, or perhaps it is better off without them. Take risks and trust your first instincts. You will be surprised and amazed at the freedom that working this way can give you.

7. Take photos or make sketches before moving any pieces so that you can replace them if you are not happy with the repositioned pieces. Once you are happy with the final layout,

above Some suggested layouts for you to try. Experiment by moving pieces around on a design wall until you are happy with the layout before stitching together.

right and below left Snake in the Grass (right) and detail (left) by Stephanie Pettengell shows how you can use commercially dyed batik fabrics with your indigo or Procion MX dyed shibori. Clever, raw edged, twisted tucks, add surface texture. Machine pieced and quilted.

leave the room for a few minutes. Walk back in and see if you are still happy; if not, move things around again. Keep going like this until you are completely satisfied with the arrangement of fabrics.

8. Now start piecing it all together. Take a close look and plan the areas that have to be joined first to make larger units. Try to avoid having to piece parts of seams to make things fit and don't forget to add seam allowances of at least 0.5 cm (¼ in) all round. Press seams to one side or open flat, whichever you prefer.

9. Once all the piecing is complete, decide if there are any areas that would benefit from some appliqué. If so, consider doing this now. If not, layer up your work using the wadding (batting) and a piece of backing fabric; pin and tack, or pin the layers together.

10. Now quilt. If you prefer to work by hand, try the Japanese sashiko style (big stitch quilting); it works well with shibori designs. Alternatively, free-machine quilt using good quality threads: Madeira and Superior are my preferred choices. Try combining machine and hand stitching in some areas; use some of the wrapping or space-dyed threads if they are the correct colour. Emphasize some of the linear type designs with couched threads, again by machine or hand stitching. Attach beads if you think the design would benefit from their use.

left *Mood Indigo* (detail) by Wendy Mose shows good use of the 'splash' shape for heavy machine quilting and the use of seeding stitches to add texture; machine pieced, hand dyed in indigo, machine and hand quilted.

right *Reflections VIII*. This detail shows the machine quilting on hand-dyed indigo *arashi* shibori; cotton and cotton/silk mix cloth.

11. Finish off the edges. This could be a raw edge, traditional binding, a faced binding or machine couching with a thick cotton yarn twice around the raw edges.

12. Finally, make a hanging sleeve and attach it to the back of your hanging; most important of all, label, sign and date your work and get ready to start all over again!

left Conflict of Interest by Pauline Adams uses the dramatic contrast of the rust-coloured fabric with the pale indigo-dyed shibori; machine pieced and quilted.

right *Sea Spray*
by Janice Dent is
skillfully worked in
fine, loose weave
cloths. The use of
raw edges and hand
quilting adds texture
to the piece; indigo
dyed cotton cloth.

left and right Two in *Blue* by Pauline Lindsay again uses the rust-coloured contrast to great effect on these two pieces, made to hang apart, but in the same room; machine pieced, hand quilted, indigo dyed cottons.

Acknowledgements

Contributors

Thank you to Barbara Corbett, Sue Hickman, Cheryl Jackson, Margaret Starr, Joan Randall, Cherry Vernon-Harcourt, Pauline Lindsay, Janice Dent, Pauline Adams, Wendy Mose and Stephanie Pettengell of New Horizons Textile Group, Alex Rankin, Annette Morgan, Claire Higgott and Jan Myers-Newbury for their quilts. Leslie Morgan for her fabric. Ken-ichi Utsuki and Hiroshi Murase for the wonderful shibori they have produced and to Delia Copland for allowing me to use her indigo dyeing instructions.

Thanks

My sincere thanks go to all of the following; to Jan Myers-Newbury for introducing me to shibori, Yoshiko Wada for the historical knowledge I have gained as a result of her definitive book, Michelle Griffiths, the UK contact for the World Shibori Network and to Creative Exhibitions for their continuing support in the field of textile art and craft. To Viv Arthur and Kevin Mead of Art Van Go for their friendship, support and enthusiasm. Thanks to Barbara Weeks, Judy Fairless, Jan Beaney and Jean Littlejohn for tutoring me and encouraging my development in textiles, and The Quilters' Guild of the British Isles. To Tina Persaud and Kristy Richardson at Batsford and Michael Wicks for his superb photography and finally to all my friends in the quilting world, including all the students I have taught over the last 18 years, but especially to Magie Relph, Kathy Colledge, Jean Kent and Linda Libby.

Bibliography

Books

Balfour-Paul, Jenny, *Indigo*, British Museum Press, 1998
Brito, Karren, *Shibori: Creating Colour and Texture on Silk*, Watson Guptill
    Publications Inc., 2003
Clarke, Duncan, *Colours of Africa*, Parkgate Books, 2000
Gillow, John, *African Textiles: Colour and Creativity Across a Continent*,
    Thames and Hudson Ltd, 2003
Gillow, John and Barnard, Nicholas, *Traditional Indian Textiles*, Thames
    and Hudson Ltd, 1993
Picton, John, and Mack, John, *African Textiles*, British Museum Press, 1989
Prideaux, Vivien, *Indigo Dyeing*, Search Press Ltd, 2003
Wada, Yoshiko Iwamoto, *Memory on Cloth: Shibori Now*, Kodansha Europe, 2002
Wada, Y, Rice, M, and Barton, J, *Shibori: The Inventive Art of Japanese Shaped
    Resist Dyeing*, Kodansha Europe, 1999

Websites

World Shibori Network: www.shibori.org
Arimatsu Shibori Museum, Japan: www.shibori-kaikan.com

Suppliers

Fabric

The African Fabric Shop
19 Hebble Mount
Meltham, Holmfirth
West Yorkshire HD9 4HG
www.africanfabric.co.uk

Doughty's
3 Capuchin Yard
Hereford HR1 2LR
www.doughtysonline.co.uk

The Silk Route
Cross Cottage
Cross Lane
Frimley Green
Surrey GU16 6LN
www.thesilkroute.co.uk

Testfabrics Inc
PO Box 26
415 Delaware Avenue
West Pittston, PA 18643
tel: 001 570 603 0432
www.testfabrics.com

Thai Silks
252F State Street
Los Altos, CA 94041-2053
tel: 001 800 722 7455
www.thaisilks.com

Wolfin Textiles Ltd
359 Uxbridge Road
Hatch End
Middlesex HA5 4JN
www.wolfintextiles.co.uk

Dyes and auxiliaries

Art Van Go
1 Stevenage Road
Knebworth
Hertfordshire SG3 6AN
www.artvango.co.uk

Dharma Trading Company
Box 150916
San Rafael, CA 94915
tel: 001 800 542 5227
www.dharmatrading.com

Dick Blick
Box 1267
Galesburg, IL 61402
tel: 001 800 828 4548
www.dickblick.com

G&S Dyes
250 Dundas Street W., Unit 8
Toronto, Ontario M5T 2ZS
tel: 001 800 596 0550
www.gsdye.com

Jacquard Products
Rupert, Gibbon & Spider
PO Box 425
Healdsburg, CA 95448
tel: 001 800 442 045
www.jacquardproducts.com

Kemtex Educational Supplies Ltd
Chorley Business & Technology Centre
Euxton Lane, Chorley
Lancashire PR7 6TE
www.kemtex.co.uk
www.textiledyes.co.uk

Threads

The Handweavers Studio
29 Haroldstone Road
London E17 7AN
www.handweaversstudio.co.uk

Inca Studio
10 Duke Street
Princes Risborough
Buckinghamshire HP7 0AT
www.incastudio.com

Antique textiles

Adire African Textiles
Duncan Clarke, Stall 10/11
113 Portobello Road, London
(Saturday 8am – 3pm only)
www.adireafricantextiles.com

Joss Graham Oriental Textiles
10 Eccleston Street
London SW1W 9LT
tel: 020 7730 4370

jossgrahamgallery@btopenworld.com

John Gillow
Cambridge, UK
tel: 01223 313803
by appointment only

Martin Conlan
Slow Loris
65, Annandale Road, Greenwich
London SE10 0DE
tel: 020 8858 2114
email: slowloris@dsl.pipex.com

Japanese textiles

www.japanesetexstyle.co.uk
www.kimono.or.jp (in English)

Ken-ichi Utsuki
Aizenkobo Workshop
Nakasuji Omiya Nishi Iru
Kamikyo-Ku Kyoto 602-8449
Japan
http://web.kyoto-inet.or.jp/people/aizen/

Helen Smith
www.clothaholics.com

Index

Adire alabere 17, 18, 20, 21, 41
Adire oniko 19, 20, 21
Africa 16
Arashi shibori 7, 12, 66–77, 83,
    101, 118
Arimatsu 8, 11, 15, 40

Bandhani 24–27

Crackle shibori 36, 37, 98

Dida 16, 23
Dyeing techniques 98
    Immersion 102
    Indigo 108
    Space 104

Equipment
    shibori 29, 31
    dyeing 100

Garra 16

Health and safety advice 101, 108, 109
Honeycomb shibori 34, 35
Hosoito ichido kairy (diagonal *arashi*
    shibori) 70–73
Hosoito yoko kairy (horizontal *arashi*
    shibori) 74–77

India 24
Itajime (clamp resist shibori) 75, 77–85

Japan 11

Kamosage knot 29, 33
Kanoko shibori 6, 7
Karamatsu (larch shibori) 12, 45–47
Kekka (clamp resist) shibori 15, 78

Kola nut 16, 17, 39, 90
Kosode 11
Kuba 16
Kumo (spider web) shibori 11, 29, 33

Maki-age (stitched and tied shibori) 14,
    61–65
Maki-nui (oversewn stitched) shibori
    56–59
Mal-mal 24
Mokume (wood grain shibori) 22, 42, 43
Murase, Hiroshi 87, 92–95

Naname goshi (lattice) shibori 80, 81
Ne-maki (tied resist) shibori 32
Noren (Japanese door hanging) 50, 64,
    65
Nui shibori 41

Obi age (kimono wrap) 6, 7, 10
Odhni 24
Ori-nui (running stitched) shibori 52–55
Osubamaba 21

Procion MX dye 32, 35, 49, 51, 53,
    66–70, 73, 75–77, 81, 83, 89, 91,
    99–105
Quilting
    Hand 37–39, 50, 60, 64–66,
        70, 72, 90, 96, 97, 107, 110,
        111, 113, 118, 121–123
    Machine 35, 37, 39, 55, 60, 66,
        68–77, 82–85, 90, 107, 110–120
    Sashiko 50, 64, 65

Rangara 24
Rasen (spiral or shell shibori) 10, 28, 33

Shibori sampler project 114–118

Shiboru 11
Shirokage ('white shadow' shibori) 12
Suppliers 126

Tenugui 11
Tesuji (pleated and bound shibori) 86–97
Tritik 16, 41

Utsuki, Ken-ichi 9, 12, 40, 42, 86, 108

Yanagi (willow shibori) 12, 86, 92–95
Yokobiki dai (shibori stand) 29
Yukata 8, 9, 11, 12, 29, 40, 42, 86, 108